Y0-BCR-909

BEYOND DEATH

BEYOND DEATH

What Jesus Revealed
about Eternal Life

Flora Slosson Wuellner

UPPER
ROOM BOOKS®
NASHVILLE

BEYOND DEATH: *What Jesus Revealed about Eternal Life*
Copyright © 2014 by Flora Slosson Wuellner. All rights reserved.

No part of this book may be reproduced in any manner whatsoever without written permission of the publisher except in brief quotations embodied in critical articles or reviews. For information, write Upper Room Books, 1908 Grand Avenue, Nashville, TN 37212.

The Upper Room website: www.upperroom.org

UPPER ROOM®, UPPER ROOM BOOKS®, and design logos are trademarks owned by The Upper Room®, a ministry of GBOD®, Nashville, Tennessee. All rights reserved.

Scripture quotations are from the New Revised Standard Version Bible, copyright © 1989 National Council of the Churches of Christ in the United States of America. Used by permission. All rights reserved.

Cover and interior design: Nelson Kane

LIBRARY OF CONGRESS CATALOGING-IN-PUBLICATION DATA

Wuellner, Flora Slosson.
  Beyond death : what Jesus revealed about eternal life / Flora Slosson Wuellner.
    pages cm
  ISBN 978-0-8358-1318-1 — ISBN 978-0-8358-1319-8 (mobi) — ISBN 978-0-8358-1320-4 (epub)
  1. Jesus Christ—Teachings. 2. Future life—Biblical teaching. I. Title.
  BS2417.F7W84 2014
  236'.2—dc23

                                                                          2013030737

Printed in the United States of America

CONTENTS

All things have become light,
never again to set, and the setting
has believed in the rising.
This is the new creation.

—Saint Clement of Alexandria

ONE

Death: What Can We Believe?

"If I go and prepare a place for you, I will come again and will take you to myself, so that where I am, there you may be also."

—John 14:3

A FTER THE STORM, the pain, and the hopeless sorrow of so many, Jesus came to Mary early in the morning as she wept in the burial garden. Quietly he spoke her name. It was he, himself, yet strangely more than himself. He came in newness, in the serene power of his love and purpose. He calmed her in her overwhelming shock of recognition, then sent her on the earth-changing mission: "Go to my brothers and say to them, 'I am ascending to my Father and your Father, to my God and your God'" (John 20:17).

She ran swiftly, the first missionary, to his frightened friends in hiding and told them, "I have seen the Lord." For two thousand years Mary and millions like her are still telling us,

"The Lord is risen!"

We Christians call ourselves an "Easter people." Together we say, "The Lord is risen indeed!" But then our unity falls apart. Perhaps no other Christian doctrine (other than that of Jesus' nature) has become so divisive and controversial as that of eternal life. Our questions show our deep perplexity and fragmentation: What is eternal life? Is it the same as life after death? Does life after death exist? How do we rise again, in body or in spirit? What is the Final Judgment? What are heaven and hell? Are the dead and the living in touch? Above all, what did Jesus say about these urgent questions?

Jesus said very little. We wish he had said much more. But the implications of what he did say are profound in power and significance. We need to look carefully at his words and stories, connecting them with the implications of other words and stories. But we need also to look at more than words. What was he saying through his healings, his way of relating to others, his choices and priorities? We need to look at his whole luminous life to begin to see eternal life through his eyes.

Mentally, I have been writing this book for over fifty years. I had been a pastor in Chicago for several years. Drained by nonstop needs in this inner-city parish, neglect of personal spiritual renewal, loss of boundaries, and extreme fatigue, I was in a faith crisis. In the midst of a funeral service for a young man of our congregation, I realized with great inner shock that I did not believe Fred was still living beyond death. Obviously I did not dump this awareness on my grieving congregation. Nothing would have been crueler. I finished the service appropriately, went home, sat down, and tried to understand what had happened to my faith. Fifty years ago there were few spiritual resources to which pastors could turn when in faith crisis. We were not supposed to have faith crises! Or if we did, we kept them to ourselves.

Fortunately, I was due for a leave of absence that was to begin in a few months. I completed this phase of my ministry, hanging on in a kind of mental, spiritual fog. God carried me through, and apparently my loving congregation noticed no difference in me or in my pastoring. At least, no one said anything. Looking back, I would not be at all surprised if some of the more intuitive members did notice something amiss and were praying for me.

During my leave of absence, which I extended for several years, my uncertainties and questions grew in intensity, but I did not really begin to face my questions with full, articulate honesty until March 1961. That day I had read the newspaper account of a great tragedy in Wisconsin—the death of a pastor and his six children in an auto accident while his wife was helping at a church event. The news item described his wife sitting in her accustomed pew while the seven caskets were brought down the aisle at the funeral service, from the largest one holding her husband's body to the smallest holding baby John, six months old.

I had never met this family, but I have never forgotten them and have often prayed for this woman, bereft in minutes of all those she had loved the most.

I wish I could tell her that reading and praying about her tragedy changed my life. Now was the time I knew I must face that empty place within me and work it through. I remember the angry thoughts and questions that rose swiftly within me: *I may be an ordained minister and parish pastor. I have had what is thought to be an adequate theological education. But in not one of my classes was the question ever raised about what happens to us after death. This woman has lost her whole family! Where are they now? Are they anywhere? I don't know. I am angry that I don't know!*

Were her husband and children obliterated as individuals?

Did "eternal life" only apply to their quality of daily living? Did they live only in her memory and by their influence for good? And what meaning does that have for a baby who has not lived long enough to have influence?

Or were these family members alive in some vague, misty condition in some far-off dimension totally unrelated to this world? Were they asleep in the grave until a judgment day at the end of time? Perhaps they were swallowed up in heavenly glory with their earthly identities lost in bliss? Were they near her in any real way, loving her? Was it appropriate or safe for her to reach out to them? If so, in what way?

Ministers in our mainline churches seldom talked about these hard questions. Funeral sermons were vague on these points and heavily larded with quotations. When we ministers talked among ourselves, there was an unspoken impression that such concerns were rather childish, even vulgar. We should stress love and life in the here and now. Eternal life is now. Never mind what happens after death.

Other people whom I questioned also offered vague answers and seemed uneasy, as if I were asking details about their surgeries or their financial situations. I heard a hilarious story around that time: A man nags his friend to tell him what he really believes about life after death. Finally his exasperated friend snaps: "Well, naturally I believe that when we die we enter glory, bliss, and infinite joy. But I do wish you would not bring up such unpleasant subjects!"

What deep inner conflict often exists between the formal teachings of our creeds and what we are actually feeling! We take the words we hear "on faith," without truly thinking about them. But unease and uncertainty linger within us.

Others were only too eager to give answers—rigid, judgmental answers—based on the belief that we are given only this one short life to deserve heaven or hell. Such teachings are widespread and are often thought to be what all Christian churches believe and teach.

I asked myself if other options beside vague generalities, on the one hand, and beliefs of a static heaven and hell on the other, existed. Was there something real and solid on which to build, something that brought together the love and justice of God and the complex realities of our human condition?

Of course, I did know some wise, compassionate people who were at peace with these questions. Some of them claimed to have personal experiences of life beyond life, but I didn't listen to them. I knew how easy it is to rationalize, to project our wish images onto our thinking. Was there any solid evidence to back up their supposed experiences?

Sometimes I asked myself if it mattered at all. Isn't it enough to live a good and loving life now and leave the rest to God? Does it really make a difference in our daily life what we believe about life after death? Shouldn't we concentrate on making heaven in this world with compassion and justice and let the next world (if there is one) take care of itself? If eternal life begins right now in this life, does it matter what happens after death?

Another serious question I had to face was whether emphasizing life after this life trivializes death. Was there not more dignity in letting a life when it ends stand as it is in the grandeur of its poignancy? If there has been tragedy, a slaughter of the innocents, let the facts stand in bareness without diluting the moral outrage. If there has been creative fulfillment, let the monument of that creativity stand in splendor without addenda, a witness to the ages. To tack on talk about more life would be like adding a cheerful ending to a Shakespearean drama.

These are powerful challenges. Scripture itself says much more about justice and mercy on earth than it does about life after death. Some books in the Bible never mention it at all!

But the questions kept coming, not only *within* me but also *to* me. I kept hearing and seeing the anguish so many people feel.

"My wife has just died. Is it possible that I will ever see her again? When the brain dies, doesn't the person die too?"

"My daughter took her own life. She had clinical depression. Is suicide unforgivable? Is she lost forever?"

"My father was never baptized, never converted. Is he in hell?"

"After my son died, he came to bring me comfort. But since I've been taught that we don't rise again until the Final Judgment, I'm afraid it was a demon pretending to be my son."

"My mother is in heaven, I know. But it all seems so misty and far away, out of touch. Does she still care about us? Does she know what we are doing?"

"My husband died last year. Sometimes I feel him close, but I don't reach out to him. I'm afraid I'll hold him back spiritually."

I have heard these cries from the heart during all my years as a minister. What responses are we ministers giving? So often through the two thousand years of Christendom, churches and spiritual teachers have brought anxiety, fear, misery, and despair to their members in insensitive, even frightening, teachings about eternal life. Many still do. I believe that the risen, living Jesus Christ who walked in the garden that Easter morning finds appalling what is often taught in his name.

It matters what we are taught and believe about eternal life. It matters in our daily lives. When a loved one dies, it matters whether he or she is gone forever, whether the lovability, the special thoughts and gifts, the precious unique individuality are wiped out for all eternity. Try to tell the parents of a little child who died that it trivializes death to believe their child still lives and is close.

It makes a radical difference in our inner peace whether or not we believe that disbelievers, suicides, or members of a different religion will be separated from God's love forever, plunged into endless pain.

It matters if we believe that a near-death experience of heaven, a vision, or some contact with a loved one who has died are hallucinations or even demonic temptations.

It certainly matters to us personally, unless we are deceiving ourselves, whether or not our own personality will be obliterated at death. Is it really enough to live on in the memories of others if those others also will someday be obliterated? Is it enough to say that we have added to the knowledge and goodness of the human race since eventually the human race and the world itself will die?

So my earnest search began. I listened (for a change) to the experiences of others. I read and researched not only what theologians said but even more what physicians, nurses, physicists, psychologists, and astronauts had to say. I studied many carefully recorded experiments. I reflected more thoughtfully on many of my own experiences.

Above all, I turned again to the four Gospels to see what Jesus is reported to have said about eternal life and to discern the implications of those sayings.

I focused on Jesus—not on Paul, Peter, James, John, or the John of Revelation, much as I honor them. I learned from Jesus' acts and relationships as well as his spoken words that what he called eternal life is meant to begin in this life and includes the life after death. Eternal life means our intimate, living relationship with God encompasses this hour, this day, this life, and the life to come.

What I have discovered and am still discovering has changed everything for me: my relationship with and trust in God, my understanding of scripture, my ministry, my way of praying. It has transformed my attitudes toward others and toward myself. It has changed my whole life.

MEDITATION

"I give them eternal life, and they will never perish. No one will snatch them out of my hand."

— John 10:28

I offer all meditations only as suggestions. Do not push yourself to follow them. If at any point you feel uncomfortable or resistant, you are free to stop or move into some other form of prayer or meditation.

Make your body comfortable, whether sitting up, lying down, standing, or walking. Do whatever feels best.

Take a few slow, deep breaths. Then move into your normal breathing, gentle and rhythmic. If you wish, gaze at something that has beauty and meaning for you: a candle, a cross, a picture, a figurine, a flower, a tree. Or just close your eyes restfully.

Think of the strong, loving closeness of God—perhaps as surrounding light, a color, enfolding wings, gentle hands holding you safely. Or you may wish to envision Jesus sitting or walking with you. Or does a word or phrase come to you? "Breathe on me, breath of God" or "Holy Spirit, fill me now." Something else?

Restfully wait in quietness, breathing in God's presence. Let your bodily muscles release, relax....

This may be enough for you today...just resting on God's strength, breathing in God's breath....

But if you feel ready, think of or picture Jesus coming to Mary on the resurrection morning, quietly speaking her name. Think of him speaking your name also as you join them there.... Feel the rising sun bathing you with warmth. Breathe in the freshness of the morning air.... Perhaps this is enough....

Do you wish to say something? ask something? The risen Jesus looks at you fully. Do you wish to share a feeling? Perhaps a hurt, a sorrow, a fear, a doubt, or a thank-you? Express what you feel with openness, honesty, in whatever words you want. Or without words, just give the feeling or problem to the risen Christ....

Do you sense a response? a touch?....

If there is only a peaceful silence, rest in that silence.... Rest in the Presence.... It is the silence of love.

It is the silence that says, "I hear you. The answer, the guidance, is forming within you now and will come forth."

As you slowly emerge from your meditation, know that a profound part of you is forever in that garden. You can return there consciously whenever you wish.

When you are ready, breathe slowly and deeply a few times, gently massage your face and hands, open your eyes, and reenter the world around you.

TWO

Death Is Not the End

"He is God not of the dead, but of the living."
—Mark 12:27

M Y HUSBAND AND I loved our friend. Not only was he
brilliant and renowned in his profession, but he was
also kind and generous. It was a joy to share his creative
thinking and his unique personality. He died after several
years of dementia in which he lost his ability to recognize,
remember, respond. His was a double death; first his brain,
then his body.

What has become of our friend? Did this double death of
his brain obliterate him as a person? Is that unique mind gone
forever? Is it possible to awake again as an individual person
after the bodily systems close down?

Many doubt with sadness that possibility, including many ministers and theologians. I too doubted it for a time. In Jesus' time
also there were spiritual leaders who doubted it. The Sadducees

were among them. They were an influential group of Temple officials and theologians who taught that because the first five books of the scriptures, the Torah, did not mention an afterlife, it did not exist. The afterlife condition known as Sheol, referred to in later scriptures, meant either oblivion or a shadowy remnant of the whole person.

"You are quite wrong," Jesus said bluntly to the Sadducees. "As for the dead being raised, have you not read in the book of Moses... how God said to him, 'I am the God of Abraham, the God of Isaac, and the God of Jacob'? He is God not of the dead, but of the living; you are quite wrong" (Mark 12:26-27).

It is clear and definite in all four Gospels that Jesus believed in and taught that individuals survive after death. He not only taught it, he also demonstrated it, rising in the power of his personhood after death, his presence witnessed by hundreds. Paul himself saw him and heard him when wide awake on the road to Damascus and much later wrote the following to the Christian church in Corinth: "He appeared to Cephas, then to the twelve. Then he appeared to more than five hundred brothers and sisters at one time, most of whom are still alive.... Then he appeared to James, then to all the apostles. Last of all, ... he appeared also to me" (1 Cor. 15:5-8).

Some Christian leaders believe, however, that the stories of Jesus' resurrection are only metaphors for the awakening of the human spirit in this life or metaphors for the birth and rising of the Christian church itself, the body of Christ on earth.

As I mentioned in the first chapter, I was thoroughly confused myself. So were many of my fellow pastors. Many of us had been taught that the immortality of the soul was a Greek concept that had nothing to do with the Christian concept of resurrection. But did the one necessarily exclude the other? Not according to Jesus.

Was there any modern scientific evidence to back up Jesus'

certainty? To my amazement, I discovered there is enormous evidence that I had never bothered to explore and research, evidence never discussed in my theological seminary and never preached about in most churches.

I began to read the meticulous record keeping of over a hundred years of the Society for Psychical Research in both the United States and Great Britain. I read the analyses by William James and Frederic Myers. I studied the experiments of J. B. Rhine at Duke University. I plunged into the later accounts and analyses of near-death experiences by such scientists and researchers as Charles Tart, Raymond Moody, George Ritchie, Kenneth Ring, Morton Kelsey, P. M. H. Atwater—among many others—and met and corresponded with some of them. I was astounded by how many modern physicists, physicians, and psychologists were immersed in these studies.

In the light of a vast body of evidence, I turned to some of my own experiences in childhood and youth whose significance I had not really explored. For example, my younger sister and I began mind-reading games just for fun during our adolescence. It soon became clear that she was the sender and I the receiver. Sometimes we would experiment by being in different rooms, so there would be no unconscious whispers or lip reading. We experimented with other people present and several times with a whole group thinking of the same number or image. Fairly soon I was sensing (not guessing) three-digit numbers correctly, as well as vivid images. It was a lot of fun.

But what was going on here? What did it all mean? We didn't reflect at depth. We grew up, went about our lives, and the games drifted off. But during my faith crisis years later I explored the reality of thought transmission. I discovered that extrasensory perception has been thoroughly studied and documented in controlled scientific experiments, far beyond our parlor games. I realized that human consciousness is not dependent on the five senses alone.

There were other experiences. Sometimes as a child and then into adulthood my consciousness would leave my physical body for a short time while I was resting, though awake. I would find myself in another place, fully aware and embodied—though in a different way. This body could move with incredible swiftness and go through walls and ceilings. I had never heard about such experiences, let alone read about them. I thought I was the only person who ever did this and found the experiences disconcerting, to say the least. I never discussed them with anyone, nor did I try to do anything exciting when out of the body. I was only eager to return to my usual state.

Years later I came across accounts of other people who had had such "excursions." I looked up books and scientific experiments on the subject and realized, astonished, that thousands of people all through recorded history had had similar experiences. I asked myself what about our human condition enables us to be conscious and aware when outside our physical bodies. And what then does this tell us about our consciousness after death?

I had not analyzed other strange events, such as the time I sat in church before the service began, and someone laid an affectionate hand on my left shoulder. I turned to smile at whatever friend had come into the pew behind me. There was nobody there!

I remembered too the night I sat in shock alone in my bedroom closet, door closed, while my beloved grandmother was dying. Suddenly I realized someone had come to me through the closed door. I saw and heard nothing, but I felt someone taking hold of my cold hands in a warm, strong clasp, pulling me to my feet. Warm and empowered, I was able to open the door and walk out.

I am thinking of an aunt, a practical, efficient postmaster of a large city, who told us how her husband who had died young had come to her several years after his death. She had not been especially thinking of him that day, but all at once he was with her, looking young and well. He smilingly talked with her for a short while. She was fully awake at the time. It was a spontaneous event and happened only once.

Literally dozens of people—rational, intelligent people I know well—have told me of comparable experiences. Usually they shared their stories hesitantly, fearing others would question either their sanity or their integrity.

Evidences such as these are important. I feel inwardly impatient when people say to me, sighing, "I wish I had your faith!" Many are actually implying, "I wish I could also fool myself with daydreams or rationalizations!" True faith does not believe something just because it makes us feel comfortable or because someone told us so. Genuine faith means a trustful commitment based on the strong evidence that the trust is deserved. I had faith in my husband's love not just because he told me he loved me and therefore I ought to believe it; but because he proved it through the hours, days, and years with loving, thoughtful actions and the integrity of his choices.

Jesus strongly believed in the importance of evidence before we commit our faith: "Beware of false prophets, who come to you in sheep's clothing but inwardly are ravenous wolves. You will know them by their fruits. Are grapes gathered from thorns, or figs from thistles?... A good tree cannot bear bad fruit.... You will know them by their fruits" (Matt. 7:15-18, 20).

When Jesus' cousin John the Baptist was in prison, he sent a message to Jesus asking if he, Jesus, was the Messiah or not. Jesus did not reply, "Yes, I am the Messiah because I told you so, and you ought to believe it." Neither did he reply, "Yes, I am the Messiah, because someone has to be, and inwardly I am convinced that I am the one—therefore you should be convinced too!" Instead, Jesus pointed to the evidence: "'Go and tell John what you hear and see: the blind receive their sight, the lame walk, the lepers are cleansed, the deaf hear, the dead are raised, and the poor have good news brought to them" (Matt. 11:4-5).

Doubts are healthy and honorable. No one should feel ashamed of having doubts. For most people, doubts result from a desire for integrity and clear thinking. The refusal to look at, sift, explore the evidence is neither healthy nor honorable. It is astonishing how many otherwise intelligent people firmly state not their doubts but their disbelief without ever having probed or investigated the evidence. When Louis Pasteur urged fellow scientists at least to look through his microscope to see the microbes for themselves, one prominent physician refused the invitation because he knew he would find nothing there!

I did finally look. Perhaps my looking took longer than would be necessary for many other people. I think I was suspicious of my very desire to find something through the microscope. But the evidence I found (and am still finding) is overwhelming. We live in a vast, complex, evolving universe in which all the signs point to intelligence, intentionality, and the unique importance of conscious awareness that enfolds and outlasts the physical form that it wears in the three-dimensional physical universe.

What is this aspect of the human being that does not depend on the three dimensions and the five senses? A huge body of material from before the Christian era and extending to modern times bears witness to the existence of a spiritual energy body, a field of vibratory light surrounding, nurturing, renewing, penetrating our physical body. Sensitively perceptive people can sometimes actually see it shining through our bodies. Some artists saw it and painted it as halos. In modern times it is often called the aura. This is not mere "New Age" teaching. It is ancient perception. When Jesus' "face shone like the sun, and his clothes became dazzling light" on the Mount of Transfiguration (Matt. 17:2), this was his own spiritual body united with God's own light.

In the thirteenth century, Meister Eckhart, a Dominican priest and renowned spiritual leader, expressed it this way in a sermon:

[T]he Scriptures say of human beings that there is an outward man, and along with him, an inner man. To the outward man belong those things that depend on the soul but are connected with the flesh.... Within us all is the other person, the inner man, whom the Scripture calls the new man, the heavenly man, the young person.[1]

When our physical body dies, drops off, we will find our conscious awareness centered in this body of light in which we have always lived, our sense of identity and memories intact. This is the experience and witness of countless men and women who have had out-of-body or near-death experiences.

When our creeds speak of the "resurrection of the body," they mean the wholeness of a person's unique identity is not only transformed by God in this life but also survives physical death. The wholeness of our personhood, our identity, includes our conscious awareness, our memories, our pattern of responses and choices. These are expressed, manifested through our physical bodies while in this world but are located, centered in our spiritual body of light that continues to grow, to learn, to act after the physical body withers and drops off.

These perceptions, for which there is increasing evidence, make many Christians nervous. But there is nothing whatever unscriptural about these realities. On the contrary, the evidence of the existence of our spiritual body of light explains many events recorded in scripture. This light is the eternal gift with which God endowed us, making us God's immortal children whose choices and growth matter so much (see Rom. 2:7; 1 Cor. 15:53-54).

But what about those such as our friend of whom I wrote at the beginning of this chapter, a friend whose mental decay we grieved? While he was still alive his brain deteriorated, causing him to lose his memories and his ability to recognize beloved friends. Does this mean that his identity had died also? Where was his spiritual body of light while this most tragic of all illnesses occurred?

It is hard to accept that physical brain cells can become ill, malfunctioning just like any other organ of the body. So far, the onset and progression of dementia is incurable, just as childhood diabetes, some forms of cancer, hydrophobia, and many other illnesses used to be incurable. Someday, with the help of God, we will learn how to prevent and cure dementia the way we have learned to prevent and cure so many formerly fatal diseases. But no matter what now destroys our physical brain and other bodily organs, our spiritual body of light cannot be destroyed.

If we try to send an e-mail through a computer, and the computer is dysfunctional, the message will not arrive. But the person trying to send the message is still alive and present. If we try to play the piano, but half the keys are dead, then no matter how fine a musician we may be, we cannot express music through that instrument. But the pianist has not vanished or died.

In the same way, when our deep self tries to communicate through a broken brain it cannot do so fully. Like a sophisticated computer, our physical brain is a transmissive organ—not a generative one. It does not create consciousness or identity; in this world it transmits them. But our spiritual body of light, which uses the brain and the five senses in this world, is not gone, lost, or dead. It lives forever.

However, I am in danger of being too glib and superficial with the analogies of the computer and piano blocking the fully alive operator. They bring up images of our conscious self being angry, frustrated at being trapped, caged in a malfunctioning machine. Though some people in coma or speech paralysis say later they were fully aware of all that was going on, most people are probably in a state of dulled consciousness, half asleep. Our surface awareness is closely intertwined with the physical brain and is usually in a clouded condition if our brain is not fully functioning. But when death breaks the connection with our organic brain, our deep conscious awareness awakens fully, as when we wake after a night's sleep.

If our loved one is in a coma or suffers from dementia, we can sit near and hold hands with our friend as we describe the events of the day, share our thoughts, express our love, and continue thinking of this dear person as the unique, precious person he or she has always been. It is quite possible that those who seem asleep are hearing us at a deep level, are aware of us and loving us.

It is even possible, if the coma is profound or the person near to death, that the eternal spirit is already released from the body. We can speak with awe of the great spiritual adventure our dear one is entering and the welcoming light that awaits. We can release our beloved to go forth with joy into greater vistas and fuller ways of loving.

Will our beloved ever return to earth in what we call reincarnation? Many believe and hope so, especially if our loved one is dying when still young or has lived an unfulfilled life. Some schools of thought in Israel in Jesus' time believed this. Some early Christians also agreed. Jesus never talked about that prospect from what the Gospels tell us. The one possible reference is found in Luke's Gospel: "Jesus... asked [his disciples], 'Who do the crowds say that I am?' They answered, 'John the Baptist; but others, Elijah; and still others, that one of the ancient prophets has arisen'" (Luke 9:18-19; see also Matt. 16:14).

So the doctrine of reincarnation was familiar, but we do not know what Jesus believed about it. Perhaps it is enough for now to understand that we continue to learn and grow in God's universe and that forever we were and will be God's unique child.

MEDITATION

We know that if the earthly tent we live in is destroyed, we have a building from God, a house not made with hands, eternal in the heavens.... so that what is mortal may be swallowed up by life.

—2 Corinthians 5:1, 4

Rest quietly in whatever way feels best. Breathe slowly and deeply a few times, then relax into normal breathing. Gaze at something living: a flower, a shrub, a tree, a bird, grass—or perhaps your own hands. Or close your eyes and touch your hands, face, or your heart area....

Picture or simply sense the breath of God breathing through these living cells...or the light of God flowing gently through the living being like a strong but gentle river...sustaining... renewing the life with warm power.... Rest quietly in this picture, this feeling....

When you feel ready, picture or just think of the outer form of this leaf, this tree or bird, your hands, your face blending into the surrounding light or living water, so that it is "swallowed up by life"....

When ready, picture or think of this living being taking form and shape in the light and stepping forth, emerging in its new, immortal form, strong, vital, rejoicing....

Has someone you loved died? Long ago or recently? Picture or think of that dear one no longer old and weak but rather clothed with radiant joy and strength....

When ready, think of your own strong, immortal body of

light within and around you...radiating through your own physical body, alive, sustained by God forever.... Rest in this thought....

When you feel ready, gently massage your hands and face in love and awe. Stretch...gently return to your daily interaction.

THREE

Resurrection Now, or at Judgment Day?

"Truly I tell you, today you will be with me in Paradise."
—Luke 23:43

IKNOW I WILL SEE my husband again on the final Day of Judgment at the end of time," a widowed friend said to me sadly. "But it may be eons, millions of years until then. In the meantime, he is asleep in the grave. He is not aware of me and my love. It seems so long to wait."

An extraordinary number of Christians believe this. Many churches firmly teach that we wake from death only at the Final Judgment. Many Christians in the early days of the church believed this also, as did many Jewish teachers in Jesus' time. It is also true that passages in the Epistles as well as in John's Revelation indicate this doctrine (1 Cor. 15:52; Rev. 20:5, 12). But what did Jesus believe? Did he teach immediate awakening after bodily death? Did he believe in the Final Judgment? He believed in both!

Jesus believed in immediate resurrection after death or he would not have promised the dying man on the cross next to him that they would be in Paradise together that very day. On the Mount of Transfiguration, he saw and spoke with both Moses and Elijah (Mark 9:2-4). They obviously were alive and awake before any Judgment Day. Jesus told Lazarus's sister Martha that she did not need to wait for the final Day to see her brother again: "I am the resurrection and the life. Those who believe in me, even though they die, will live, and everyone who lives and believes in me will never die" (John 11:25-26).

Paul, in his letter to the Philippians, reflects, "By my speaking with all boldness, Christ will be exalted now as always in my body, whether by life or by death. My desire is to depart and be with Christ" (Phil. 1:20, 23). This verse clearly implies immediate life after death.

But if we live immediately after death, what is the meaning of all the passages in scripture about Final Judgment? As I read through the descriptions of the end-time and Final Judgment attributed to Jesus, I do not find that he definitely and clearly equates the Judgment with the first and only raising of individuals who have died. His parable in Matthew's Gospel that tells of the nations gathered before God and the separation of the sheep from goats is about communal groups, institutions, and powers, and their survival or destruction (Matt. 25:31-46).

When Jesus describes a calling of the elect from all corners of the earth on the final day (Mark 13:27), he may be referring not to individual people awakening from death but to all the powers, all the people in the created universe who will be present for the final summation.

In John's Gospel, when Jesus speaks of raising his believers on the last day (John 6:44, 54), he may well mean that for each of us our last day of earthly life is our "last day." In this same chapter he says, "I am the living bread that came down from heaven. Whoever eats of this bread will live forever" (John 6:51). The ultimate last Day of creation, whenever that may be, is not the same as our individual wakening after bodily death.

Jesus seriously warns us against trying to predict when the final cosmic transformation will come: "But about that day or hour no one knows, neither the angels in heaven, nor the Son, but only the Father" (Mark 13:32). It is astounding how often would-be prophets from shortly after Jesus' death to the present have ignored this warning!

The apocalyptic passages in the Gospels can be interpreted and understood on several levels. Given the omens Jesus foresaw, possibly mingled with later eyewitness descriptions, some texts seem clearly to describe the sacking and destruction of Jerusalem. Jesus grieves over that suffering to come, especially for the suffering of women and their babies—homeless, freezing in the winter (Matt. 24:15-21).

Other scriptures speak of wars, earthquakes, famines, floods, and devastating plagues (Luke 21:10-11), all of which have been true in the history of the world since its beginning.

The descriptions include planetary, cosmic disasters: "There will be signs in the sun, the moon, and the stars, and on the earth distress among nations confused by the roaring of the sea and the waves.... The powers of the heavens will be shaken" (Luke 21:25-26).

Someday, there will indeed be an end to our planet and our solar system. Astronomers agree on this. Whether our earth will end from solar flares, solar cooling, colliding meteors, or other astronomical disasters no one knows. We do know that in nature nothing lives forever.

Jesus knew there would be destruction of nations—even as Israel was heading for destruction—an end to our world, an end to creation. He knew there would be a final summation, a final healing, a new creation.

But the Gospels' apocalyptic words may also be interpreted in a personal way when we experience traumatic changes and cataclysms in our lives. The world as we have known it can end for us in many ways: impending death, catastrophic illness, loss of a loved one, a ruptured marriage or family relationship, a betrayal, a loss of job, a loss of trust in our church.

Sometimes our personal world's end is a slow, long attrition rather than a cataclysm: a cooling off of a treasured relationship; discovering we have chosen the wrong spouse, the wrong commitment, or the wrong job; an increasing, subtle abusiveness in a workplace.

But whether swift or slow, we do feel that our sun, moon, and stars have gone out for us. We do feel earthquakes shaking the ground we thought was solid and safe. We are bewildered, overwhelmed by the "roaring of the sea and the waves" over our heads. These are our personal end-times.

Jesus knew all about personal end-times. He had been driven violently out of Nazareth, his hometown. His mother and brothers doubted his sanity at first and tried to stop his ministry. His life was often threatened. He knew what it was to be misunderstood, lied about, hated, betrayed, let down by friends. He knew when he died he would be labeled by most of his own world as a fraud, a blasphemer, and a failure. He saw the approaching disasters for his own nation. Israel was in danger, ruled by corrupt kings, disempowered by Rome, threatened with armed rebellion by angry zealots. Severe polarization existed between rich and poor, between political and ecclesiastical powers.

How do we face our end-times? "Then they will see 'the Son of Man coming'... with power and great glory.... Stand up and raise your heads, because your redemption is drawing near" (Luke 21:27-28).

I believe these words are true not only of the cosmic end of the solar system—and perhaps the whole created universe—but also in the midst of our own personal end of our world.

What a challenge to rebirth, to transformation! During our own end-time, we stand up, raise our head, and welcome the new power, the new beginning offered us! The time of our greatest disaster is the very moment the risen Christ comes to us most swiftly, bringing the rising of a new and greater sun, a vaster light, a new and stronger ground under our feet. In short, Jesus presents us with a new creation as well as the special closeness of God's presence and empowerment.

My mother survived many failing suns and shaking grounds. She was born crippled in both feet and only with great pain learned to walk. She was left a young widow with two small children. She faced many severe health crises. In her fifties, she faced the trauma of her youngest child undergoing cancer surgery with every likelihood of dying. She knew all about end-times. She told us she had always felt the closeness of God in the midst of pain, grief, and fear and that she always knew other doors would open for her with even greater challenges of more inclusive love, more powerful gifts, swifter growth. These new doors may open for us swiftly or gradually, but open they will. The scriptures overflow with miracles of new life, hope, strength, and vision at the very point of most intense darkness.

Perhaps Jesus' supreme gift to us, even greater than his healings, is this transformation, this new life of the Spirit rising in power from the grave of the old life. I used to wonder why Jesus' first recorded miracle in John's Gospel was changing water into wine at the wedding feast in Cana. To be sure, it was a kindly act for the hosts. But was it a dignified beginning of his ministry? Surely a healing would have been more appropriate! I avoided the incident in my preaching. Later, God helped me to look more profoundly, and I realized that this first miracle was one of transformation. It symbolized the new life, the new creation replacing the old. The miracle of transformation is the central miracle throughout the scriptures!

"He found us as water and changed us into wine" is an early Christian saying.

Jesus spoke passionately about transformation—both our own and the world's—in his first sermon in the Nazareth synagogue. He had just returned from his forty days of solitude and prayer in the wilderness. During those hungry, hard days, he had struggled to understand the meaning of his deep powers, those vast God-given gifts. He knew their limitlessness, and he was tempted (as we all are) to use his powers manipulatively as ruthless shortcuts that would bring God's reign into the world by force and domination. Many passionately righteous social justice workers yield to this temptation to use mastery over others to enforce their own vision and thus become demonic themselves.

But through those days of lonely inner struggle, Jesus realized that God's realm comes through inner transformation, through hearts opening to love, mercy, and the honor of freedom of choice. He faced his hometown friends and his family and told them why he was in the world, quoting from Isaiah's words:

> *"The Spirit of the Lord is upon me,*
> *because he has anointed me*
> *to bring good news to the poor.*
> *He has sent me to proclaim*
> *release to the captives*
> *and recovery of sight to the blind,*
> *to let the oppressed go free,*
> *to proclaim the year of the Lord's favor...."*
> *Then he began to say to them,*
> *"Today this scripture has been fulfilled in your hearing"*
> (Luke 4:18-19, 21).

Release, setting people free, healing their wounds, and above all proclaiming "the year of the Lord's favor" are what Jesus brings us from God. The year of God's favor was the Jubilee Year. In Israel's tradition, every fifty years the nation would set aside a year of God's special closeness and mercy. The Jubilee opened with the sound of the shofar, the ram's horn, which was blown at special times of God's deliverance and transformation. It was blown at Mount Sinai when Moses received the Law. It was blown as the call to war and at the end of war. (I heard it once, when visiting our local synagogue at the end of the Vietnam War. The sound is not beautiful; it is greater than beauty. The sound is electrifying. It is *radical* in the full sense of the word—grasping our very roots!) When Israel blew the shofar from the Temple walls on the eve of the Jubilee Year, it signaled the time when all slaves were set free, prisoners released, debts forgiven and canceled, and arable land allowed to rest and recover.

When Jesus proclaimed that now, this very day, began the Jubilee Year, he was, in effect, blowing the shofar. The people did not need to wait fifty years. They did not need to wait until the angel Gabriel blew the ultimate shofar at the end of time. *Now,* Jesus said—this very moment—God offers the great transformation. It can begin now in your heart, your home, your community, your nation. God forgives your past and releases you from its bondage. The gift is here. The doors stand open. A new creation awaits you.

What does all this have to do with death and judgment? It means that when Jesus spoke in eschatological language about the end-time and Final Judgment, he meant not only the end of the world, the end of time and space and the created universe, but also that each new day, each new moment is our personal judgment day. God is saying to us, "This very hour I offer you a new life, a new beginning, a transformed heart. If you accept, you will become a new creation." Theologians call this "realized eschatology," which means the end-time, the Final Judgment, has been with us all along.

A year ago during Advent, I bought a foot-high statue of Gabriel, the angel of the shofar; the angel who told Mary of the Incarnate One to be born through her consent; the angel who, tradition says, will sound the final trumpet at the culmination of all things. This Gabriel statuette is not pretty, not sentimental, not simpering. Gabriel strides forward, his cloak blowing behind him as if in a high wind. His tall, powerful wings are poised for flight. His gaze is focused, intent, and his arms are raised high as he blows the trumpet.

I did not pack away this statue with my other Christmas decorations. I have kept it in a place where I can see it every day of the year, every hour of the day. When I look at it, I remember that this very moment the shofar, the trumpet, sounds. At this moment, I can raise my head and welcome the year of Jubilee. At this moment, Christ comes "with power and great glory" (Matt. 24:30), offering me transformation. Today is my Judgment Day and resurrection combined.

Those whose bodies have died have risen too. They too discern the meanings and aims of their earthly life. All of us will be together at the culmination of time, space, history, God's universe. But we do not need to wait until then. We all are alive and together now, and our love flows like a river between us through God, who "is God not of the dead, but of the living" (Matt. 22:32).

MEDITATION

Your sun shall no more go down, or your moon withdraw itself; for the LORD will be your everlasting light.
　　　　　　　　　　　　　　　　　　—Isaiah 60:20

Rest your body peacefully or take a quiet walk. After a few slow, full breaths, breathe gently, thinking of the river of life flowing through your whole body.... Let your weight rest on the ground beneath you... rest more completely on God's everlasting arms, infinitely stronger than the ground....

This is the strength, the light that will never fail. These are your new sun and moon, which never go out.... It may be enough for now just to lean on this power, breathe in this eternal light....

But if you feel ready, let your memory go to a time when you felt your earthly lights go out... a time when the ground shook under you. You are looking at this time from within Christ's protection. You are safe. What steadied you at that time? What help came to you? What guided you, strengthened you, gave you hope?... Reflect on this.... Did God come to you through a special person? several persons? a community? a certain book? music? art? a garden? nature itself? special creative work? a powerful purpose? an inner place of strong peace?... These are ways by which God touched you and brought you forth.

Do you sense a change in yourself since then? a newness? What has changed within you?...

When ready, reflect on any present difficulty: a problem to solve... a hurt that needs healing... anger... anxiety... sorrow... illness... a pending change.

Christ is with you in "power and great glory" (Matt. 24:30)....
A newness is offered...a clearer air to breathe...a deeper
insight...a profounder healing...an ending...a beginning.

A new sun and moon to walk by. A resurrection now...a
mystery opening....

Breathe in the promise. Sense your body filling with peace....
When ready, return slowly from your meditation, gently massag-
ing your hands and face.... Stretch, then move into your daily life.

FOUR

What Is Heaven?

"In my Father's house there are many dwelling places."
—John 14:2

"MANY DWELLING PLACES." What spacious words! They give us a feeling of heights, depths, variety, new horizons. Jesus knew all these dwelling places intimately. They were his home. During his earthly life, he breathed their air and walked in the strength of their beauty, embraced in their love.

Jesus gave us few details about these dwelling places. His earth's mission was to bring heaven, the fullness of God's realm, into our daily lives, relationships, choices. Perhaps he also hesitated to dwell on heaven's descriptions because he knew they would fall so short of the reality.

Those who have had an experience of heaven when near death, out of the body, or in a vision agree that it is impossible to describe accurately what they saw, heard, and felt. They tell of light far beyond earthly light. They speak of colors—colors far more beautiful than those of our earthly spectrum. They have experienced love, but love more profound and more transforming than we have ever known. They try to describe the swiftness of motion, the intense activity, the excitement of discovering and creating, the vistas of adventures into the depths of God's creation in all its dimensions.

Since these people have no adequate words, they have to use symbols and metaphors to reach our understanding. Their efforts are like trying to describe to a young child how it feels to be married to your beloved or communicating the thrill of a symphony concert, surfing great waves, or completing an intense, fascinating project. You would have to say, "Remember how you felt when you learned to ride your tricycle? How do you feel when you go to your best friend's house for the day? How about when they bring in your birthday cake with all the candles? What's the feeling when you wake up Christmas morning?"

Paintings, poems, and hymns have tried to describe heaven through metaphor, image, or analogy for centuries. The symbols so often chosen may sound boring or downright weird to us in our time, but they carried meaning, comfort, or motivation for earlier centuries. Resting on clouds was an exquisite thought for generations of laborers who worked from dawn to dark without respite. Fresh white robes were a distant dream for those who owned only their worn, stained work clothes. Flight on swift wings was a thrilling idea for people in the pews who seldom traveled beyond their own village and then in a slow, jolting ox-cart on a muddy track. Harp music and vast singing choirs was a rapturous thought for those villagers whose only experience of music was their own singing in the village church or tavern.

In my girlhood we often sang that ancient virile hymn, "Jerusalem the Golden," written by Bernard of Cluny in AD 1145. The third verse especially struck me as strangely irrelevant for the twentieth-century teachers, lawyers, doctors, and shopkeepers singing in church:

> *And there, from care released,*
> *The song of them that triumph,*
> *The shout of them that feast;*
> *And they, who with their Leader*
> *Have conquered in the fight,*
> *For ever and for ever*
> *Are clad in robes of white.*[1]

Exciting, I thought. *But it sounds exactly like a Viking feast, full of shouts, songs, and ale-filled mugs (horns?) thumping the tables after the day's battle!* Probably that is exactly what it was!

The apostle Paul did not even try to describe his own experience of heaven in metaphors. He tells us about it in halting, almost stumbling words, quite different from his usual eloquence:

> *I know a person in Christ who fourteen years ago was caught up to the third heaven—whether in the body or out of the body I do not know; God knows. And I know that such a person—whether in the body or out of the body I do not know; God knows—was caught up into Paradise and heard things that are not to be told, that no mortal is permitted to repeat* (2 Cor. 12:2-4).

Permitted or not, it is beyond our ability to tell not because it is too vague and unreal but because it is so astoundingly real that earth's realities dim in comparison.

Many years ago I had a dream filled with strong images and metaphors of one of those dwelling places of heaven. It felt more like a vision than a dream though I was asleep at the time.

Sometimes we do have visionary dreams that we never forget and that strongly influence our life and thoughts. Usually they are dreams of intense color and meaningful coherence, not the usual jumble of fragments. I believe God speaks to us through such dreams, as God so often did in biblical stories.

This dream came to me several years after the death of Fred, the young church member of whom I wrote in chapter one. I had kept in touch with his parents by mail, but since my husband and I had moved we met only once before Fred's mother died also. We lost touch with his father, and as time went on I thought of them only occasionally but with affectionate wistfulness.

One night, in my dream, I found myself visiting a dwelling place full of light of a soft brilliance I had never seen before. It was the home of Fred and his mother, who welcomed me warmly and showed me their rooms. I do not remember any details of our conversation except that it was friendly and relaxed, as if we had never been separated.

In one room, Fred had set up some kind of scientific experiment (he had been heading for medical school when he died). He was fascinated with this work. His mother, who on earth had always worn dark, conservative clothes, was now dressed in a long gown of glowing colors that floated around her as she walked. She moved with grace and freedom unlike the slow, stiff walking I remembered. The house was spacious, but I saw no bedrooms. I asked where they slept; they only smiled without answering.

I went to one of the large windows overlooking a garden and opened the window. The air that flowed in was so vibrantly strong and fresh that I could almost feed on it. I looked out into the garden and saw something so indescribably beautiful that the shock of its beauty woke me up. What was it? I do not know. I have no metaphor.

Fifty years later this dream remains strikingly fresh in my memory. It came to me when the concept of heaven was still vague to me and long before books on near-death experience began to appear.

I sensed through this dream that the heavenly dwellings are indeed many—many layered, multidimensional. After our bodies die, we will find ourselves in surroundings that feel natural and homelike to us. As we grow more fully into joy, empowered love, and wider understanding, we will be invited to other, vaster vistas brimming with vital purposefulness, adventure, spaciousness. We are not "laid to rest," as death announcements and funerals put it, but are inspired to choose creative work that we love so much it does not feel like work but instead like divine passion.

It is not a matter of higher or lower. I don't believe that such hierarchical thinking exists in God's love, which is fully with us at each stage of our growth. We are as delighted with our child's first fumbling independent step as we are when he or she walks up to receive the graduation diploma.

I have never liked the old saying, "God is easy to please but hard to satisfy." I believe that each step of growth, each expanding awareness and wisdom, is fully satisfying to the One who loves us infinitely. From that delighted satisfaction comes our power to keep growing and exploring new dimensions. Even when we reach the dimensions of the highest angels, God will love us not one whit more than God loves us now. The only change is that we become more aware of God's love already embracing us and are more able to respond to that love.

Jesus wanted us to become conscious of the deep unfolding of our own spirit while still in our earthly bodies. Many people feel anxious at the thought of spiritual growth and change in the same way that the thought of life after death is frightening. Will these changes be scary plunges into utter strangeness? Will we become unrecognizable saints, no longer interested in ordinary daily life? Will we be thrust into dimensions and demands too big for us? Will we shrivel at the enormity of feeling God's presence more keenly?

Another visionary dream came to me about fifteen years after my dream of heaven. This new dream showed me through powerful symbols the merciful nature of our spiritual growth within God's love.

In this dream I found myself alone, standing on the surface of a strange planet. In the traditional science-fiction manner, I said loudly to the landscape, "Take me to your leader!" An enormous green giant, who looked about a mile tall, came up over the horizon. He had a kind face and said in a friendly way, "I have come to take you to the leader." I thought to myself, *If this messenger is so terrifyingly tall, just think of what the leader must be like!*

"How will you get me there?" I asked timidly.

"Oh, I will pick you up and carry you in my hand." I felt as if a Redwood tree had offered to pick me up. I have a bit of difficulty with heights.

"Is there any *other* way I can get to the leader?"

"I will go and inquire," he said, smiling indulgently and leaving the scene.

In the next sequence of the dream, I found myself sitting in a small, rather cozy spaceship. The pilot, a pleasant-looking man about my height, was at the controls. We chatted together for a while, and he showed me how some of the controls worked. Finally, I asked who he was. "I am the leader," he answered, smiling.

I stared at him, amazed. The leader? Not a huge, scary giant but someone my size, someone friendly, someone with whom I felt completely at home.

"Glance out of the window if you want to see how high we have really come on this journey," he added.

I looked down. We were hundreds of miles high, far higher

than the giant. So high, and yet I was not afraid! So far below, all over the planet's surface, many lights spelled the Latin word *amor*, "love."

I think it was first of all a visionary dream of God's incarnation through Jesus—God no longer a fearsome, menacing mystery but One who shares our joy and pain; a God who understands our fears, temptations, and human frailty; a God who asks us not to fear as we worship but to love.

What God is in ultimate fullness we cannot now know. A young child taken into a cathedral cannot discern the complexity of its design, let alone the years of its envisioning and planning. Nor can the centuries of thought and faith it represents even enter the mind of a child. But I well remember when I first saw a cathedral as a child. Its vastness, its heights awed me; its color and beauty entranced me; its funny little carvings under the choir seats delighted me; but above all, I felt safe there. In spite of all the as-yet-unknown mystery around me, I felt wrapped in protecting warmth. I felt at home.

The dream told me that even as God is friend in spite of all the mystery, so also are spiritual change and growth. With each new step forward, we will enter more deeply into our home. We will become more who we really are, not less. We may reach heights we had never dreamed of, but within God's merciful *amor* we will reach these heights by ways that seem natural at heart, even when new and exciting.

We are not shown or asked to envision God's full plan for us. An acorn is not shown the full-grown oak tree. "Beloved, we are God's children now; what we will be has not yet been revealed" (1 John 3:2). It is enough to know at this point that each new door and each vision that opens for us will lead us to a vaster home—but still a home.

Jesus gave another brief but significant description of heaven that has been widely misunderstood. This misunderstanding has led to much emotional suffering: "When they rise from the dead, they neither marry nor are given in marriage, but are like angels in heaven" (Mark 12:25).

I have heard more than one sorrowful widow or widower say sadly about this text, "If there is no marriage in heaven, that means I can't join and live with the person I loved best in the world." Once an elderly priest said to me with great poignancy, "I promised my church I would never marry, and I have been faithful to my promise. But in my heart I have often been very lonely. Do you think Jesus means that I will never have a loving soul mate, either in this life or the next?"

I do not think Jesus meant this at all. When he made that remark, he was responding to a frivolous test question put to him by some Sadducees. They denied the existence of life after death and hoped Jesus would make a fool of himself. They asked him what would be the marital status of a widow who married seven brothers, one after the other as each one died. In the life to come, to which of these seven men would she be given as wife? One can almost hear the laughter of those standing around listening at the absurd possibilities of the ludicrous situation.

As usual, Jesus' unexpected answer ignored traditional responses and struck straight at the root of the matter. Obviously, she would be "given" to no one! She would no longer be anyone's property. Like the angels, she was free to follow her heart's deep choice. This was radical. Marriage in Jesus' time had nothing to do with preferences and love between the spouses. It was a family decision involving property ownership, dowries, birth of heirs, and so on.

This was the usual basis of marriage up to fairly recent times. Free choice was not an option. The bride to be was the last person to be consulted, if she was consulted at all. Her father, or another male guardian, had the legal right to choose her husband and give her to him after finances and property issues were settled. She went from one ownership to another. A remnant of this long tradition still persists in some marriage ceremonies. It was almost universal when I was a girl. "Who gives this woman to be married to this man?" the minister asked. "I do," replied her father, putting her hand into the hand of the bridegroom. Of course by then it was just a symbol with no legal force behind it, but still a significant symbol.

Never did Jesus say that we could not join or find our beloved in heaven. On the contrary, we will be set free from the rigid legalities so often found on earth. In every way we will be released to follow our heart's deepest longings, like "the angels in heaven."

If we have found our soul mate while on earth, of course we will be joined in heaven. If we on earth have never found our heart's partner, we will find that one in heaven. Loneliness does not exist in those "dwelling places" of which Jesus spoke. We will say with Robert Browning (1812–89), who found his life's companion and completion in his wife, Elizabeth:

O thou soul of my soul! I shall clasp thee again,
And with God be the rest![2]

Jesus' descriptive words about heaven are few indeed. But their profound significance always implied release, freedom, expansiveness, joyous intensity, and a multidimensional realm.

We see the same witness in Jesus' actions and ways of relating to others. The will and the realm of God that he longed to bring into our daily lives on earth always included this release, expansiveness, and inclusiveness. He made it clear that in God's realm there were no dividing walls between men and women, between young and old. This was radical teaching in his time, when strict rules separated the genders and the dignity and rights of children were almost nonexistent.

Jesus welcomed and included all races and cultures. He gave healing and guidance to Gentiles and pagans as well as to Jews and the orthodox. He shared time and healing concern with a Syrophoenician woman and a Roman centurion. He recognized no impassable barriers between himself and those considered heretics, such as the Samaritan woman with whom he talked at the well. A "good Samaritan" businessman became the model of courageous compassion in his most famous parable.

Jesus gathered into his warmth those whom orthodoxy labeled as outcast sinners to be avoided. He touched and let himself be touched by those whom society condemned as impure and contaminating, such as the bleeding woman. He gave healing attention to a crippled, bent-over woman in the middle of a synagogue worship service. He treated destitute beggars with dignity.[3]

Jesus emphasized that what flows from the heart is what matters most to God. We are set free to make choices and to set others free also to choose. We are free to speak to God from our hearts without intermediaries. We are given freedom to thrust aside the walls of exclusion and give healing love directly to one another.

This is God's realm, already at work on earth in the way yeast works within dough and the way living seeds thrust upward from within the earth. This is heaven, beginning now. We are invited, called, challenged to enter this realm of heaven while still embodied on earth. This is why Jesus came to us—to open the door of this realm and call us to enter.

Bodily death will not disrupt this reality. Rather, we will know a continuation and a vast deepening beyond description of what we had already begun to experience on earth. This is the feast, the bread and wine that Jesus offers to share forever.

MEDITATION

"Abide in me as I abide in you.... Abide in my love."
—John 15:4, 9

Let your bodily muscles relax, release their stiffness....
Breathe gently, slowly. You are breathing God's air.... God's light
and warmth embrace you.... You are at home in God's heart
now....

What images come to mind when you think of heaven? A
green pasture or hills? a calm blue ocean? flying? great moun-
tains? a radiant cathedral? a chorus of soaring music? Or is it a
feeling of infinite space, overwhelming love, a sense of oneness?...

When ready, think of experiences you have had that brought
this sense of heaven even in the midst of daily problems and
struggles.... Experiences of profound peace...inner joy...aware-
ness of loving unity with others...oneness with God...awesome
beauty...creative action...your deep self, vibratory with life....

Reflect on these times and experiences.... What do they tell
you about God and God's realm?...

Is there anything in your life now that touches on heaven? If
there is no sense of heaven on earth for you at this time, do not
dwell on guilt. Share honestly what you feel with God. Ask God
to show you any block.... Do you sense what the block may
be?...Ask what can be done....

"Abide in me, as I abide in you," God says to us through
Jesus. In what way can we enter more fully into relationship
with our life's Source?...

Again, God says through Jesus: "I have said these things

to you so that my joy may be in you, and that your joy may be complete" (John 15:11). This joy is what God desires for us in our heart's center, beginning now and continuing into life beyond death, for all eternity.

Ask God for the joy that is in Jesus....

Breathe gently and calmly. God has heard your prayer. Heaven's light begins to unfold within you. Welcome this light.... Breathe it.... Let it embrace you....

Come forth slowly from meditation, gently reenter daily life, knowing a change has begun at your center.

FIVE

What Is Hell?

"While he was still far off, his father saw him and was filled with compassion; he ran and put his arms around him and kissed him."

—Luke 15:20

I WAS TEN YEARS OLD when I went with my family to see the Sistine Chapel of the Vatican in Rome. Along with my family I was stunned, fixed by the power of Michelangelo's paintings all over the chapel's ceiling. Then we gazed at the huge centerpiece over the altar showing the Last Judgment and the separation of the saved souls from the damned who were cast into hell.

I remember the shock I felt as I looked at the stern condemnation in the beautiful face of Jesus and his hand lifted in harsh and total repudiation of the lost souls as they fell away from the light. No hope. No mercy for all eternity! On our travels we saw the same theme repeated endlessly in stone carvings, paintings, stained-glass windows: the hopeless anguish on the faces of the condemned and the cold, relentless judgment on the faces of Jesus the Savior and the saints.

Of all church doctrines taught through the centuries, that of endless hell and the condemnation of a wrathful God has caused the most horror, terror, and suffering. Most of our Christian denominations taught this doctrine up to fairly recent times, including my own church! In the early 1700s, Jonathan Edwards, Congregational minister and revered theologian, preached a sermon titled "Sinners in the Hands of an Angry God." In this long sermon, preached to a congregation that included terrified young children, Edwards asked his shuddering people to picture themselves hanging like a loathsome spider from God's reluctant hands while God decides whether or not to drop them into hell's eternal flames—flames that they thoroughly deserved!

Most of our mainline churches no longer preach this doctrine, but many churches worldwide still do. We find these concepts in popular movies of the supernatural and in cartoons showing stout men warily eying leering demons with pitchforks. (Similar to the cartoons of heaven with equally stout men holding harps instead of cringing from forks!) Whether in laughter or fear, we are all familiar with the images of hell.

What are these ancient images telling us about God? Is this God of wrath the same God who loves us with an everlasting love? Would we mortals send anyone to eternal torture, let alone someone we love, no matter what they had done? Does this mean we are more merciful than God? Or is this doctrine of an endless, hopeless hell a supreme insult to the God we see through Jesus?

And yet, Jesus did speak of those dark, fiery dwellings called hell as a terrible reality. He spoke of them quite often. One of his parables inspired Michelangelo's painting of the Last Judgment. What are we to think? Are we followers of one who taught of

God's infinite, parental love but also of a God who might send us to endless torture? How can we love or trust such a God?

Many of us ministers of the mainline churches avoid coming to grips with this impossible dilemma and ignore those scripture passages about hell. I certainly avoided them during my years as a parish pastor. But later I realized that if I were to remain a minister, a teacher of prayer and spiritual growth based on Jesus' teachings, I had to research those scriptures, think about them, and above all pray about them.

When I finally prayed about the meaning of Jesus' words on hell, I felt a powerful response rising within me. I did not hear words, but I sensed someone was responding in this way: "Yes, Jesus was a realist. He knew well the rotting, destructive face of evil. He knew that the hellish state of mind can and does exist in this life and can exist beyond death. But nowhere does he teach that any individual soul is forced, doomed to stay in that condition for all eternity."

I inwardly sputtered, *But what about that story he told, found in Matthew's Gospel, that story that inspired Michelangelo to paint his Last Judgment?*

> *When the Son of Man comes, . . . all the nations will be gathered before him. . . . The king will say to those at his right hand, "Come, you that are blessed . . . for I was hungry and you gave me food . . . I was a stranger and you welcomed me. . . . I was sick and you took care of me, I was in prison and you visited me." . . . Then he will say to those at his left hand, "You that are accursed, depart from me into the eternal fire prepared for the devil and his angels; for I was hungry and you gave me no food. . . . I was a stranger and you did not welcome me, . . . sick and in prison and you did not visit me." . . . Truly I tell you, just as you did not do it to one of the least of these, you did not do it to me" (Matt. 25:31-36, 41-45).*

The answer that came surprised me. I looked again at the words: "all the nations will be gathered before him." Nations! This is a parable, a story about communities: nations, governments, political parties, racial and cultural groups, corporations, workplaces, churches, family clans, neighborhoods.

These communal bodies are judged according to their awareness of and attention to the needs and suffering of the vulnerable members among them. If communal groups neglect or abuse the powerless, suffering ones, they will not survive as powers in the world. Eventually they will weaken within, disintegrate, and perhaps even vanish, as have many powerful nations, kingdoms, empires, and communities of all kinds. This is a ruthless fact of history.

Perhaps Jesus was thinking of the story in the book of Daniel. All Israel knew this story well. It tells of the merciless king of ancient Babylon, Belshazzar. Cruel, wasteful, contemptuous of justice and compassion, he gave a great orgiastic feast. In the midst of this festival, a mysterious hand appeared and wrote on the wall the words: "MENE, MENE, TEKEL, and PARSIN." Only the prophet Daniel could interpret these words: "God has numbered the days of your kingdom and brought it to an end;... you have been weighed on the scales and found wanting" (Dan. 5:26-27). Belshazzar's kingdom began its collapse. Some corrupt communal bodies quickly disintegrate. Others slowly fragment and die. Still others may continue to exist as a remnant with a weak identity, but their former vast power is gone.

The biblical word *cursed* does not mean that God hates a communal group or an individual. It means God has withdrawn a special power, a God-given gift, a mission, and given it to another because that power had been ignored, neglected, or abused.

Communal powers are more open to corruption and evil than are individuals. The mob-spirit, for example, is a combined emotional force of the whole community that sweeps along individual people to feel fury and commit acts they would not have done on their own. The methods of thought control a community uses quickly overwhelm the judgment and resistance of most of its members. The communal power develops a persona of its own and becomes the only reality for individuals who live within it. We have seen this happen in great nations as well as in small cults. A communal persona can overpower members of a family, a church, a workplace. All our communal groups must be alert to the potential writing on the wall: What is my group doing to its members? Is there freedom, compassion, justice?

But besides communal judgment and condemnation, what did Jesus say about individual persons whose lives have been corrupted and who find themselves in a hell of their own making? He uses a powerful parable:

> There was a rich man who was dressed in purple and fine linen and who feasted sumptuously every day. And at his gate lay a poor man named Lazarus, covered with sores, who longed to satisfy his hunger with what fell from the rich man's table.... The poor man died and was carried away by the angels to be with Abraham. The rich man also died.... In Hades, where he was being tormented, he looked up and saw Abraham far away with Lazarus by his side. He called out, "Father Abraham, have mercy on me, and send Lazarus to dip the tip of his finger in water and cool my tongue; for I am in agony in these flames." But Abraham said, "Child,... between you and us a great chasm has been fixed, so that those who might want to pass from here to you cannot do so, and no one can cross from there to us" (Luke 16:19-26).

This parable was already an old, widespread story found in rabbinic writings as well as in earlier Egyptian literature about the judgment of the dead. Jesus repeats this story, showing his passionate concern for the pain of the powerless and his hot anger at those who are merciless in their power.

At first reading, there seems to be little hope for redemptive change. The rich man (named Dives in later traditions) appears to be trapped forever in his fiery pain. His abuse of Lazarus was not overt abuse apparently. It was a more devastating abuse, an abuse that indicates a spiritual blinding and hardening: he never really *saw* Lazarus! This sick, starved human being lying near his doorstep was just street furniture, something to step over as he hurried on to more important things. Perhaps this blindness of the spirit, this total unawareness, is the sin most difficult to heal whether in a community or an individual. I read somewhere recently that without awareness, redemption is impossible.

But this is the paradox: once we begin to realize our blind, indifferent neglect of those in need and pain, then begins the flame of remorse that we call hell. We have all felt at least a touch of those flames: the memory of withheld tenderness, the cold shoulder, the put-down, the contemptuous look or word, the helping hand withheld, or, worst of all, the unnoticed suffering.

I am thinking of a recent inner "Dives" choice in my own life. I was standing at a counter in a grocery store waiting to give my order. A woman came up beside me, also waiting. I had noticed her earlier: hair dyed a glaring blonde with dark roots showing, garish jewelry, layers of almost clownlike makeup, a raddled face. With distaste, I chose not to look at her. She glanced at me once or twice, but I chose not to return the look—no meeting of eyes for me!

Driving away, I began to realize what I had withheld during that encounter. I could easily have given her a friendly smile, eyes that acknowledged our shared humanness, her essential dignity. I chose to be unaware that her face showed her life had been a hard, wounded one.

Would a friendly glance have changed her day, made any difference in her life? Who knows? But difference or not, I had withheld humanity. I had "grieved the Spirit." Other chances will be given me to share the human touch, but that particular chance is gone forever. It is too late to change that bit of history.

Someone has said, "Hell is truth seen too late." Am I exaggerating a trivial incident? I don't think so. Any deliberate loveless choice, no matter how brief, is of hell's essence just as any choice of human compassion is of heaven's essence. But we can learn from our moment of hell and turn around. No one dooms us to remain in that state.

When theologians and preachers of former generations spoke of hellfire, they really meant actual flames devouring a body constantly renewed to feel the torture. But what would be the point of burning anybody for all eternity if he or she is still unaware of the real significance of what has been done and left undone? There would be no point; nothing would be essentially changed. It would be mindless, meaningless torture going on forever. Only when awareness of the horror they have committed dawns in the hearts of the abusers does the fire begin.

But now the deeper, divine paradox reveals itself. At the very moment our agonized awareness of the suffering we have caused begins, the door of redemption opens. It opens because at last we begin to see the truth about ourselves. The Holy Spirit can begin to work. The Paraclete (the Greek word for the Holy Spirit) means the One who stands by us and calls us forth!

In the parable, Dives awakens. He sees Lazarus at last, although far off. Dives feels the fiery pain of his neglect. The great chasm of which Abraham speaks is the chasm of the moment of choice gone by. Dives cannot go back now and help Lazarus, who was dying in the street, just as I cannot go back and give a warm smile to the woman next me in the store. That chance is gone forever and is an everlasting loss, at least until

God heals all history. The true translation of *eternal* as used in scripture is *age-long*, implying a corrective period of time.[1]

But now at least we see, we know. And that means we are changing. Dives also begins to think of others besides himself. He thinks of his brothers still on earth, perhaps as merciless as he has been. Can someone be sent to warn them?

Dives still (as we do) has so much to learn about love, about wounding and healing. He wants Lazarus to heal his thirst. How often we want the person we have hurt to help us immediately with soothing forgiveness and understanding so we won't continue to feel so bad.

Here the ancient story ends. Abraham speaks rather tenderly to the awakened, suffering Dives and even calls him "child." But the chasm is still there. Is this God's last word?

No, the ultimate last word comes in another parable, this time one of Jesus' *own* stories. This story is found in Luke 15, the chapter directly preceding the Dives and Lazarus story. This chapter has been called "The Gospel within the Gospels." It even has been said that if the whole Bible were lost but this one chapter remained, it would tell us all we need to see into the heart of God.

This is the chapter of lost things—grieved over, passionately sought, and found at last. Jesus tells three stories: a lost coin (probably a precious bridal ornament) and the woman who loves it, who sweeps the house floor all night until she joyfully finds it; a sheep that has wandered off and its shepherd who abandons everything in his search; and supremely, a beloved son, who callously takes his money and abandons his home and his anguished father who never gives up hope.

Then Jesus said, "There was a man who had two sons. The younger of them said to his father, 'Father, give me the share of the property that will belong to me.' So he divided his property between them. A few days later the younger son gathered all he had and traveled to a distant country, and there he squandered his property in dissolute living. When he had spent everything, ... he began to be in need. ... He would gladly have filled himself with the pods that the pigs were eating; and no one gave him anything. But when he came to himself he said, 'How many of my father's hired hands have bread enough and to spare, but here I am dying of hunger! I will get up and go to my father, and I will say to him, 'Father, I have sinned against heaven and before you; I am no longer worthy to be called your son; treat me like one of your hired hands.' ... But while he was still far off, his father saw him and was filled with compassion; he ran and put his arms around him and kissed him" (Luke 15:11-20).

There are fascinating parallels between the story of Dives and Lazarus and that of the prodigal son. First, both Dives and the son are cocooned in their complacent selfishness and indifference to the pain of others. Dives ignores the dying beggar in the street; the son cares nothing for his family's suffering. In Jesus' day, for a son to demand his inheritance, abandon his family, and move away to a far country was an almost inconceivable act of irresponsible contempt.

Dives and the son both live extravagantly. Then both begin to suffer; Dives, who has died, suffers from thirst and fire. The young man, still in his body, suffers from loneliness and desperate hunger. They both reside in their self-made hells.

Both Dives and the son come to some degree of awareness of what they have done and their responsibility for their conditions. "He came to himself" is a significant remark in the story of the young man. This could also be said of Dives who sees and understands. The hearts of both cry out for help. Their motives are mixed, of course. Yes, they are aware of what they have done, but mainly they want to be out of their intolerable situations. Most of our motives are well and truly mixed ones!

Dives and the son both know they are "far off." The road of transformation can be a long one. The son actually turns around (the meaning of the word *repent*) and begins the journey. But "while he was still far off, his father saw him. . . ." Dives too was "far off," but we can be sure that the Father saw him. While burning in the fire of remorse, all Dives has to do is say, "Though I have done evil, I am still God's child. I will get up and go to my father" and then turn around. We can be sure that God would run, embrace Dives, and take him home.

What about that great, fixed chasm, that lost moment of opportunity gone forever? God's love strides across all chasms. The moment is gone, but we are becoming a new creation. Through the power of God's redemptive love, through the mystery and miracle of transformation, all the moments of time will be healed. How this can be done is beyond our comprehension, but scripture promises throughout that it will be done. The same scripture Jesus read in the Nazareth synagogue at the start of his ministry contains this promise: "They shall build up the ancient ruins, they shall raise up the former devastations; they shall repair the ruined cities, the devastations of many generations" (Isa. 61:4).

When we have turned around and come home, there will still be everything to learn. Our souls have been cleansed, but our old habits remain with us. An old, pithy saying states, "I have Jesus in my heart, but grandpa in my bones!" After years of throwing his money around, the prodigal son must learn new ways of being a family member. Dives must learn to see his neighbors at all times and in all places. A new life, whether on this earth or after death, is a time of joy, yes—but also a time of learning, growing, seeing more clearly, atoning for past mistakes, opening our hearts ever wider. We will also know sorrow for past abuses until that time when God heals all things. But this sorrow will no longer be for us the fire and chains of hell.

There must be the age-long potential of hell because God gives us free choice. Since we are daughters and sons of God—not mindless puppets—God allows us to turn away, harden our hearts, and create our spiritual prisons. But God will never give up on us, never cease searching for us. This is the promise throughout the Gospels, supremely celebrated in Luke 15. Many have wondered if that pointed sentence in the Apostles' Creed, "He descended into hell," implies that Jesus went there to find Judas!

God's love is infinitely stronger than the power of our hells. Jesus said to Peter, "On this rock I will build my church, and the gates of Hades will not prevail against it" (Matt. 16:18). I had always envisioned that as hell (Hades) itself battering away at the rock of the church. But one day a minister set me straight on that point: the church itself is meant to be the divine rock that God throws at hell's doors to free those trapped there.

What a difference! God will not allow our hells to have the last word. The transforming power of God's love works radically, hurling itself against all the forces that fragment and attempt to destroy us, all that traps us in hopeless despair, all that imprisons us in resentful malevolence, all that crushes love in our hearts.

Some years ago I read an astounding second-century apocryphal Christian document, the *Acts of Pilate*. It contains a vision of Christ's radical, redemptive love released and at work within our self-made hells, whether in this life or the life beyond:

> *The Lord looked down from heaven that he might hear the groanings of them that are in fetters.... And now, O thou most foul and stinking Hell...open thy gates.... The Lord of majesty appeared in the form of a man and lightened the eternal darkness and brake the bonds that could not*

be loosed: and the succour of his everlasting might visited us that sat in deep darkness.... And lo, suddenly Hell did quake, and the gates of death and the locks were broken small, and the bars of iron broken, and fell to the ground, and all things were laid open....

And behold, the Lord Jesus Christ coming in the glory of the light of the height, in meekness, great and yet humble.... For behold now, this Jesus putteth to flight by the brightness of his majesty all the darkness of death, and hath broken the strong depths of the prisons, and let out the prisoners, and loosed them that were bound....

And the Lord set his cross in the midst of Hell...and it shall remain there forever.[2]

Why did we ever believe within this love of God that hell would have the last word?

MEDITATION

"He has sent me to proclaim release to the captives and recovery of sight to the blind."

—Luke 4:18

If anything in this meditation feels disturbing, anything you are not ready for, end it and move into some other form of prayer.

As you rest your body, take a few slow, deep breaths; then relax into your usual breathing. Lean on God's strength around you. You are in a safe place. You are in God's heart.

When you feel ready, ask the living Christ, the Healer, to bring to you the memory of a time when you felt trapped by your own actions or feelings: Smoldering anger?... Acts of unkindness?... Neglect of others?... Bad choices?... A breach of faith?... Addictive habits?... Long-term resentment?...

As you reflect, keep remembering you are not alone. The Healer is close beside you.... The love of God envelops you, no matter how completely and long you were inwardly trapped....

Return with the Healer to this present moment.... Is the weight of this memory unhealed? Are you still trapped by it in guilt, the powerlessness to change the past?... Do any new prisons of the spirit hold you?... Do you feel unfree?...

Christ the Healer gives you clearer seeing.... Do not fear the seeing.... It is the Healer who opens your eyes....

The Healer is saying,... "I see your pain, your prison. You do not have to stay in this place. I am here to bring hope... to bring release.... Trust me with your hand.... Together we will step out of this prison and go forth.... You will learn and grow.... You will be healed.... You will love more fully.... You will be made new.... Give me your hand. We go forth...."

Breathe slowly, deeply.... Slowly leave the meditation.... Stretch.... Raise your head.... The Healer walks with you into your daily life.

SIX

How Close Are We to Those Who Have Died?

Suddenly there appeared to them Moses and Elijah, talking with him [Jesus].

—Matthew 17:3

Yᴇs, ɪ ᴋɴᴏᴡ my husband is in heaven now and that I will see him again. But is he in any way near me? Does he know what I am doing? Does he care anymore about my daily life? If I speak to him, can he hear? Does he speak to me or reach out to me in any way? We were so close. What has happened to that closeness?"

The sorrow in the woman's voice made so clear that frightening finality of a beloved one's death. Many of us have experienced that severing. Just a few hours, or even minutes ago, we could hear their voices, see their smiles, feel the movement of their hands. But now, with that last intake of breath, all this is gone. The body we know and love is now inert and will never

move again. There is no more response. Where is the one we
love? Gone to a far place with no more shared daily life? no
more communication of any kind?

Many Christians are taught and believe that though their
beloved dead still live in spirit in heaven, they are totally separated
from us on earth. Contact is not possible, let alone appropriate.
We are so often told, "Your dear one is safe with God. That is all
you need to know. Release the dead totally into God's hands and
leave them there. Pick up your life, and carry on without them."

What did Jesus say about this? Again, he said very little
according to the Gospel accounts. Perhaps he took it for granted
that the "God . . . of the living" (to whom we are all alive whether
in or out of the physical body) never intended bodily death to be
a total separation from loved ones still on earth. He showed no
surprise that Moses and Elijah came to him and spoke with him
on the Mount of Transfiguration. He probably already knew
that they had loved him and had watched over him, that they
were always aware of what he said and did, that they always
prayed for him and helped guide him.

When Jesus told the Sadducees during the discussion on marriage that those who have died shall be as the angels, he implied
that when we are in our spiritual bodies of light in heaven, we can
visit and watch many dimensions of God's universe, including
earth. Both the scriptures and thousands of witnesses on earth
through the centuries tell us of innumerable human encounters
with angels and loved ones in recognizable form.

Certainly all souls are in God's hand, but that hand is not
a clenched fist. That hand does not cut us off from closeness to
those we love. That ancient phrase "the communion of saints"
means not only the saints in the church calendar but all of us who
are united in God's love. Forever we commune with one another.
Loving awareness still flows from the saints to us and from us to
them. How could God, who is love, ordain it otherwise?

This assertion frightens some people. "I am afraid I will hold her back if we remain close. Perhaps it will prevent her spiritual growth. After all, Jesus told Mary Magdalene in the resurrection garden not to hold onto him."

I have heard this kind of warning so often from pastors and counselors, and often from grieving people. But why should we think that healthy love and closeness could hold anyone back? God's hand is not a clenched fist nor is healthy love a possessive clutch. When Jesus said to Mary Magdalene on the morning of the Resurrection, "Do not hold on to me" (John 20:17), a better translation is "Do not clutch me."

Any relationship can become a clutch if the love is an anxious, codependent emotion. Such love can indeed hold another back from growing, maturing, free decision making. But unhealthy possessiveness is a disorder of love, wound-based and wound-causing. If love is healthy, however, it releases other people to their growing, their free choices. How can it possibly hold anyone back? On the contrary, warm, releasing love serves as the foundation of maturing and growing. Why should this end when the body dies?

To be sure, the kind of endless grieving that seriously disrupts daily life and its responsibilities may well hold us back whether we are the one who has died or the one who has remained on earth. But we could say the same about a mother or father who goes to pieces emotionally over the "empty nest" transition. Constantly attending séances to get nonstop messages and daily advice from a deceased loved one is a "holding back" behavior. But essentially it does not differ from phoning a parent or a best friend every day for the reassurance of hearing their voices or asking advice about every little decision. When we are trapped in this manner of crippling dependence, it makes no difference whether the one we are clutching is in or out of the body. All loss of emotional freedom is a serious disorder whether we are relating to those on earth or to those in heaven.

"But will this awareness continuing to flow between me and my loved one prevent me from new ways of life, new friendships, new loves?" is a question of real concern.

I asked my mother about this years ago. She was a young widow when she married my father. Her first husband had died of a World War I injury when they were both in their early thirties.

"Was it hard to put my father in Elbert's place when you remarried three years later?" I asked her.

"No one could be put in Elbert's place," my mother answered. "Each of us has our own special place in the hearts of those who love us because each is unique. No one ever takes our unique place. Your father also has his own special place in my heart that no one else can fill."

"But whose wife will you be in heaven?" I asked, unintentionally repeating the question the Sadducees asked Jesus two thousand years earlier (except that I was asking in good faith).

My mother shook her head. "None of us knows where our most profound longings will lead us when we are in heaven. But I do know this: genuine love does not subtract and divide. Genuine love adds and multiplies. No one will feel bereft or deprived. We all will be connected deeply by love we cannot even imagine now."

Some people feel such a depth of soul bonding with their earthly partner that they experience an eternal union. Often they choose to remain single after their beloved dies. They sense vibrantly an ongoing daily companionship but one that in no way curtails their freedom.

A dear, lifelong friend of mine experienced this soul bonding in a second marriage after years of an abusive first marriage. When she and her husband met, they sensed a powerful union, almost like recognizing someone they had known and loved forever. Their marriage of twenty-four years was a rare unity of completion and fulfillment.

Three mornings after her husband's death, my friend awoke feeling a loving kiss from him though she could not see him. Later, she felt an unexpected strong embrace from him the night before some friends they loved were killed, murdered in an African nation where my friends had served some years as medical missionaries.

"Though I could not see him," my friend told me, "he was right there with me. I was attending a play and had not been especially thinking of him at that moment. But his real presence was unmistakable. I could feel the embrace physically. It was as if he were trying to prepare and comfort me about something—I did not know what. I learned about the murders in the news the next day."

During the following years this friend has glimpsed her husband on occasion and has always felt his love and enduring companionship. When she prays each day, she senses him praying with her, especially in prayers for others. She senses that he lives a full, creative life in his dimension, just as she lives fully in hers. As a scientist and lay preacher in his church, he was always exploring the mysteries of God's creation. She knows he is still learning, exploring, helping others.

Nothing in their profound closeness holds the husband back spiritually any more than their intimacy held him back on earth when he would drive each morning to work in his medical lab. She too has never been held back. She has moved to a different location, made many new friends, remained active in church and professional work, and found new gifts and strengths growing in her. She is fully alive in this world, enjoying her life and interested in all that is going on around her.

Admittedly, such a powerful ongoing union is rare. But healthy love and friendship can manifest themselves in many other ways after death. There may be clear dreams, for example, dreams that far surpass the usual symbolic dreams, dreams in which the loved one is vibrantly with us, usually looking well and much younger.

We may experience occasional touches, as I did on my shoulder in church (described in chapter two). There may be a sudden fragrance in the room or a light turned on unexpectedly. We may hear music or feel a warm breeze. We might experience a strong awareness of guidance when confronting a problem. We may feel helped to find some important information or a lost possession. Perhaps we will be led to a certain book and open to a page containing helpful words. Often, new ideas, concepts we had never thought of, will come to us unbidden.

I too have felt the touches, heard the music, breathed the scent, received unexpected guidance and many ideas that do not seem to come from me alone. So have uncounted men, women, and children who have told me about these and other types of experiences. Often they begin the conversation with these words: "I've never told anyone about this before. They would think it was all my imagination or that I have a mental problem." Quite frequently they add sadly, "I especially did not tell my minister!" This does not surprise me, though it makes me sad too. I remember well how I would have listened and responded to such stories early in my ministry. Some ministers would rebuke and warn these people on rigidly orthodox grounds. I would have looked respectful and then said soothingly, "Well, you have been under a lot of strain recently. We often react in strange, imaginary ways. Don't worry about it; it will pass. If not, we can consider therapy." Pastors have become much more open-minded and flexible in recent years; but fifty years ago I had a lot to learn!

I believe it is better to let these experiences come spontaneously rather than to seek them out through psychic training courses. Such forms of sensitivity training are not necessarily wrong or harmful in themselves. But if a person has a wounded and dysfunctional background, such deliberate efforts can become addictive and compulsive. For example, if a person has had difficulty forming warm, close relationships, he or she might become so absorbed in trying to make otherworld contacts that daily life and human beings in this world are neglected.

If we don't experience spontaneous contact with our loved one who has died, we need not feel anxious or inadequate. It definitely does not mean that he or she has abandoned us or ceased to love us. The one who has died may need complete rest for a while or has not yet realized that contact is possible. Or it may mean that we do not have a receptivity to that form of contact. The love still flows between us even though we cannot feel it. For example, some healers feel strong, warm, tingling sensations when they lay healing hands on someone; but other healers, who may be just as effective, feel nothing special at all.

Whether or not we experience special contact, it helps to remind ourselves that the ones who have died have not broken off connection with us. We can inwardly speak to them in a natural way, share amusing events with them, occasionally read aloud the poetry or sing the songs they love, tell them they are forever part of our ongoing life even as we are part of their ongoing life. We can share and celebrate anniversaries, not in a mournful way but in joy and gratitude. We can include them in our prayers and invite them to join in our praying. We can ask them to send us their thoughts and ideas. These thoughts may come to us in the form of dreams, symbols, metaphors, slow or swift inklings—but they will come to us.

Some people receive contact but sense that it is unhealthy contact. How do we discern the health of our contact? We judge the health of our beyond-death contacts the same way we discern whether our earthly contacts and relationships are healthy: do we feel free or controlled? Are we growing in loving outreach to others around us? Is our daily life still interesting?

Do our usual activities give us energy? Do we make independent choices and explore options? Or do we feel a growing dependence, addictiveness?

Some after-death contacts should definitely be discouraged, just as some types of earthly relationships should be discouraged. Some who have died do not realize they have died or they are in a state of denial. They do not want to enter their new, wider life or perhaps simply do not understand there is a wider life to enter. They cling to their old life on earth out of ignorance, fear, anger, desire to control the living, or perhaps sheer inertia. They just want to stay where they have always been. These are the earthbound.

The grandfather of a lifelong friend was one of these "earthbound." All his life he had been a hard, compulsive worker who pulled his family into prosperity after a childhood of extreme poverty. He was not an evil man; but driven by fear of losing what he had gained, he made it clear to everyone that things had to be done his way in every detail. He maintained iron control. Bodily death did not stop him. He clung to this world. One night he came to my friend, his granddaughter, as she lay awake in bed. He told her angrily that no one listened to him anymore; everyone ignored him. Would she please do something about it!

My friend is a woman of great spiritual strength and insight and was not in the least afraid. She spoke to her grandfather lovingly and firmly. She told him they all admired him for the many good things he had done for the family but that now it was time for him to move on. She assured him that Christ awaited him, friends awaited him, and that all he had to do was turn toward the Light. He was to leave now and not come back to her with his complaints. She was tired and needed sleep. He left sulkily. She inwardly prayed for him and fell asleep. Some years later, he came to her once more. His face was peaceful. After that, he never tried to contact her again.

Another close friend had a similar experience that was less easily resolved. She and her husband had divorced a few years earlier but had remained in friendly contact for the sake of their daughter. After his sudden, unexpected death, he began returning to his family on a regular basis. They could all see him—his former wife, his daughter, his daughter's school friend. Even the dog saw him!

Her ex-husband was not angry, nor was he trying to control anyone or to reveal any information. He just wanted to stay on earth where he felt comfortable. He wanted to be surrounded by familiar rooms, objects, and people.

In life this man had been a charming, childlike, rather irresponsible person who had no desire to change anything, including himself, and no wish to explore new options. He had been vague about religion, believing in God but with no special desire to come closer to God. New life after death did not interest him. Earth was good enough for him.

My friend knew these visits were totally inappropriate. She was fond of him, sorry for him, but this situation was not healthy for any of them. Her ex-husband was not learning or growing, and his visits were disrupting their daily life. Friends, understandably, stopped coming to the house.

My friend contacted a prayer group and others she trusted who knew how to pray. She surrounded herself with God's love and light. Then she firmly told her former husband that this between-worlds way of living was unhealthy for everyone, including their daughter. These visits must stop—now. He must turn to God's Light and move on. There he would find family and friends who had died earlier. They awaited him and would welcome him to a better, happier life. She told him he could help his daughter on her earthly journey so much more by loving and praying for her in heaven.

My friend reassured her ex-husband that she and his daughter would always think of him lovingly and would always pray for him. But he must grow beyond his dependency on them and on earthly life. He tried several times to return, and she learned to be very tough with him: "This is no longer your home. We care about you, but your real home—a much better one—is waiting for you. There is nothing whatever to fear about going forward. Turn around now; leave this place. Go into the Light. God is holding your hand. Our prayers are with you. Go."

There was nothing demonic about these encounters. They required no exorcism rites. These were childish, earthbound souls clinging to what they were used to, wanting people to notice them and listen to them. They could not let go, release. They had to be dealt with in exactly the same way we would deal with a clinging neighbor who keeps coming to our house when not invited or phoning several times a day for reassurance or to talk about trivia. The fact that the people had died makes no difference in the way they needed to be encountered: with lots of tough love and firmly set boundaries.

I am horrified by the teachings of some churches that all forms of contact with those who have died are demonic. The daughter of a friend of mine once said quite seriously to her mother, "Mother, when you die please don't try to come to me. How would I know whether it is a demon in disguise come to tempt me?"

To me, this insults not only God and our love for the one who has died but also insults our common sense. How do I know that my next-door neighbor is not a demon in disguise? How about my bank teller, my car repairman, my sister when she telephones? To me, this is spiritual paranoia!

But what about true evil? Many people worry about the possibility of demonic interference in after-death contacts. Does that ever happen? Of course, it can happen, just as it can happen in earthly encounters. But most of the time "there is no one here worse than ourselves," as the old saying goes.

The Gospels tell us that Jesus did occasionally face unseen destructive, disintegrating forces. Were they independent demonic beings, or were they the combined energies of earthly malevolent thoughts and intentions that took on a life, a persona, of their own? Certainly a powerful miasma arises from inhumane communal groups that spreads dehumanizing influence far beyond its original perpetrators.

We sense the presence of evil, embodied or disembodied, by its attacks on our freedom, our ability to make independent choices, our inner vitality and hopefulness, our sense of self-worth. When we experience un-freedom, lightlessness, and energy drain in earthly relationships or those after death, obviously we must separate ourselves from them and place ourselves immediately under the Light and protection of the living Christ.

Such experiences do not necessarily mean that the "devil" is attacking us, but it can mean that a group or a relationship is exerting an energy and influence that are dehumanizing for us.

Most of the time we are dealing with human wounds. What is so often glibly termed *demonic possession*, so sensationalized in books and movies, is almost always severe clinical depression—mental or emotional illness from brain imbalances or emotional trauma. What often seem to be demonic symptoms can appear in rigidly controlling churches or mind-controlling religious groups and cults, especially those that focus heavily on fear of the devil and demonic possession. Sometimes the suppressed, angry rebellion in the hearts of the church or group members takes the form of blaspheming evil presences.

The large majority of after-death encounters have nothing demonic about them. Usually they come as a brief loving contact; an enduring, noncompulsive closeness; or a dependent childish clinging such as described in this chapter.

The contacts also often occur for healing purposes or for reconciliation. I believe that after death we grow into richer

understanding and gain clearer insight about our earthly relationships. In this life we make mistakes with other people;
often with those we love the most. We unintentionally hurt one
another because we ourselves hurt. We project our own needs
and wounding associations onto other people and then react to
those projections.

So often after someone dies, we find ourselves thinking: *I
understand it better now. I see the roots of our problem more
clearly. I wish I could return and take back what I said. I wish
I could go back and reach out a more loving hand or talk it
through together with more understanding and tenderness. Now
it is too late.* The guilt and sorrow may haunt us for years. But I
have seen healings take place after death. The one who has died
is also reviewing and reflecting on his or her life's journey, its
mistakes as well as its fulfillments.

My mother and my grandfather loved and admired each
other but always had had a difficult relationship. They were
more alike than they admitted. They kept hurting each other
unintentionally. They tried to do better. I could see them trying. They tried to be gentler, more understanding and intuitive.
Certainly there were happy times when they were together, but
all too often there would come the tactless remark, the careless
put-down, the critical comment—and then the hurt and anger,
brooded over and not forgotten.

After her father's death, my mother felt deprived and frustrated
that there had never been any full, honest discussion of the tensions
between them, no real healing or closure. It was too late now.

Three years later my mother stood in the operating room
where her youngest daughter, who had just undergone surgery,
lay near death. The doctors had permitted my mother to attend
the surgery because at one time she had been a medical student.
All at once she knew her father was present and very close to
her. She neither saw him nor heard his voice, but she knew he

was there just as surely as if he had opened the door and walked into the room. She felt the strength of his love streaming toward her and the firmness of his support.

During the long months of my sister's convalescence, my mother frequently felt her father near. She realized that the tinge of bitterness in her memories of him was gone. She began to understand his hurts and the needs of his life. She felt that he too understood hers. The powerful sense of his presence eventually faded away, but she felt a new, ongoing companionship and often an intermingling of thoughts and ideas. Healing had come to them both.

It is never too late for healing to take place in a relationship. Death need not be an obstacle. Not everyone feels the strong, actual presence my mother felt, but I have heard from so many people that they sense a new clarity, a fresh understanding. For them, mutual forgiveness has occurred and changed their lives.

I am sure this is the way God intended it. The Holy Spirit builds bridges between the estranged. Why should death build new walls of estrangement? Why should mutual healing and growing ever cease?

I do not believe that God ever intended for bodily death to be a total separation. It is a grief, an immeasurable loss when the body of our loved one dies. We cannot minimize or trivialize that anguished sense of loss, knowing we will no longer hear the voice we love, the laughter, the footsteps. But we are so much more than our bodily selves. Our deep souls need never be separated. We do not have to say good-bye, depending only on our memories to sustain contact with our loved ones. The so-called dead are as alive and active in their own dimension as we are in ours. Our love and thoughts can still flow to one another and mingle. All dimensions of heaven and earth and everywhere else in creation are held [remain] alive within the heart of God, who is the "God not of the dead, but of the living" (Mark 12:27).

MEDITATION

"Holy Father, protect them in your name..., so that they may be one, as we are one."

—John 17:11

If you do not feel ready for this meditation, leave it and pray in the way you feel guided.

Rest quietly.... Sense your muscles gradually releasing their tension.... Breathe gently, naturally.... Lean on God's close strength.

When you feel ready, picture or think of Jesus and his friends sitting together in the quiet upper room sharing supper.... They break and share the bread.... They drink from the cup.... Think of yourself sitting there with them at table.... You also drink from the cup and eat the bread.... Jesus now is praying for them, and praying for you....

He is praying that all who love him and one another will always be in deep unity...never separated in heart and soul, even by death.

When you feel ready, think of someone you love who has died, long ago or recently. Think of that person alive, well, smiling at you.... Sense his or her love flowing out to you like a strong, warm current....

Smile back at this loved one.... Let your heart open and its love flow to him or her...a releasing love that is thankful for this shared love and blessings for the dear one's new life....

Do you feel sadness or guilt for any kindness you may have withheld? Inwardly share your sorrow for this.... Share what you have learned from it....

Were there unresolved issues or conflict of some kind?... Pray that God will heal you both and help you both see the problem more clearly.... Pray for fuller understanding.... Pray that this new understanding will grow in your present earthly relationships....

Sense or think of how your loved one is growing in new ways, working with joy and creativity...healing from wounds... fulfilling hopes and dreams....

Pray to be guided to think of your loved ones in a natural way in your daily life, inwardly smiling at them often...sharing feelings of gratitude and thankfulness...sharing amusing little events...moments of beauty....

Express thanks that this dear one is forever part of your life....

Come forth slowly from your meditation, praising God whose heart holds you and your beloved friend forever in the ongoing closeness that death cannot break.

Gently massage your hands and face, open your eyes, and reenter your daily life smiling, held by God in oneness.

SEVEN

Preparing Ourselves and Others for Death

"Are not two sparrows sold for a penny? Yet not one of them will fall to the ground apart from your Father."
—Matthew 10:29

ALL AFTERNOON I had sat next to the bed of the elderly woman, one of my church members, who was quietly dying in her own home. As her pastor, I was helping her to prepare for death, but I was also preparing myself. I was only in my midtwenties, and though I had officiated at several funerals and had been with the dying just before and just after their deaths, this was the first time I had ever helped guide anyone through the dying process itself.

The woman had only a few hours left, the doctor had told me and her family. She was not at all afraid, nor was she in pain. Her breathing was slow and quiet, her face peaceful, and she slept most of the day.

Her family members came in and out of the room often, but

the two who stayed there were myself and her young nephew, about my age, who was a Catholic priest. He sat on one side of the bed in the small room and I on the other. When she would awaken briefly, I would hold her hand, say a prayer, or read aloud a scripture passage such as Psalm 23. Her nephew prayed silently. I believe he was hoping that during one of her wakeful spells she would turn to him and ask to be received back into the church in which she had been born. But he was respectful and in no way interfered with my ministry to her.

Once she opened her eyes, looked at us both, smiled, and said, "You children must be tired! You've sat with me all day. Go and drink some tea in the kitchen. I'll be fine." She drifted off to sleep again.

We obeyed her and sat sipping our tea at the kitchen table, not quite knowing what to say to each other. This was 1958, years before Catholic and Protestant clergy were completely relaxed with each other.

When we returned to her room, she smiled lovingly at us "children," slept again, and woke no more on earth. As I held her hand, looking at her face, all of a sudden her face and body became empty. It felt exactly as if a house that had been full of life and vitality was abruptly vacated, the lights turned off and the door shut. What lay before me on the bed was like a lovely gown the owner had taken off and left lying there.

As I said in chapter one, I knew little at that time about what happens after death and practically nothing about the reality of our spiritual body. I think now that my dying friend knew much more clearly than I what was happening. But I felt fully the radical, awesome mystery of death's transition. I think it likely that she prayed for me on the other side of death, which helped me a few years later to begin my new spiritual pilgrimage. I had thought I was preparing her for death. But I believe now that she was preparing me!

To prepare for death is not meant to be a grim, stoic march to the disintegration of the grave. I believe God means it to be an adventure (painful and difficult at times) of entering into the mystery and power of a new life. Childbirth is a good analogy. My first experience of preparing for childbirth powerfully grounded my understanding of the death process.

I took a childbirth training class during my first pregnancy. Class members learned ways of breathing, relaxing, and muscle flexibility that would help us work with, not against, what nature was doing through us. Above all, we were taught attitudes of positive anticipation. This was all quite new for pregnant mothers in the 1950s! I remember the instructor saying to us, "When labor begins, you will probably have several hours of increasingly hard work ahead of you. Try to think of it as if you were pulling a rope as hard as you can, using every body muscle as you strain, then rest and breathe, then strain again. But as you pull that rope, remind yourself that you are not pulling back from being dragged into a chasm of doom. On the contrary, as you pull on that rope, you are pulling toward you your life's greatest treasure, your dearest beloved, up from the cliff, and soon you will see and embrace it!"

This positive approach made an enormous difference; it gave the long, often uncomfortable, process an intense, beautiful meaning. My heavy work was bringing the beautiful treasure closer and closer to me. Easy? No! No great life-changing transition is easy: graduation, leaving home, first job, choosing a spouse or life partner, becoming a parent, packing up and moving—all involve heavy work and some painful moments. There is always effort and some anxiety as we leave the old familiar ways and lifestyles and embrace the new.

Even a wedding, a celebration of supreme joy, is after all a form of human sacrifice in front of that flower-decked altar! What are we actually doing at that altar? Giving away our lives, that's what we are doing! No more old girlfriends or boyfriends, no more cooking, spending, vacationing for our own tastes alone, no more accountability only to ourselves. Even if we have lived together with our beloved before marriage, now we are committed, presumably for life! The old is gone—behold, the new has come!

But, for the joy that is in us, for the greater joy to come, we make these renunciations with a full heart. Jesus reminds us that "the kingdom of heaven is like a merchant in search of fine pearls; on finding one pearl of great value, he went and sold all that he had and bought it" (Matt. 13:45-46).

Can the death process really be compared to these other earth-shaking transitions? Again there is danger of being glib about this question. Our physical bodies, like all physical bodies on earth, are programmed to resist death. Our powerful immune systems at this moment are waging unceasing war against all that would infect or destroy us. Nourishment, fertility, and survival are priorities in the laws of nature from earthworm to human being.

Our organic human existence and survival are extremely important in our spiritual development. Jesus healed everyone he possibly could. He never told anyone that he or she would be better off dead and in the better world beyond. Yes, there was a better world to come, but in the meantime he made it clear that bodily life is a gift of enormous significance. I think we need this world, this earthly life, to learn things that we learn nowhere else so well. Bodily life is to be cherished and valued.

To leave this world can be daunting and difficult, no matter what joy and freedom lie ahead. It cannot be easy for a baby, as the birth process begins, to be slowly, relentlessly pressed out of the safe, warm, familiar environment of its mother's body into the unknown. Does it have any awareness at all of the world of spaciousness and light that lie ahead? Does it have any inkling that loving hands and arms will welcome and hold it as it enters the mystery?

If it is twins being born, how does the one left behind feel as its close, warm, entwined sibling is taken away? Does it feel bereft, abandoned? Does the wait feel unbearably long?

Some say that our own birth may be the hardest emotional and physical experience we will ever have—leaving the only reality we know for the unknown—let alone the discomfort of the process! But I often wonder if God's Spirit somehow enfolds, comforts, and encourages us through the difficulty of being born. I have read that methods known as gentle childbirth, which include muted noise, softened lights, gentle ways of inducing breathing, immediate warmth, result in babies that don't cry after the first gasp. They have peaceful expressions on their faces and sleep more soundly. They do not register traumatic shock from the birth process.

Can we learn better how to die through reflecting on these more recent methods of childbirth for both mother and child? Can we learn ways of relaxing and releasing so as to feel anticipation? As the bodily systems of our old life close down, can we learn to sense, even though drowsy and weak, that our spiritual body of light is gathering strength to move into a vaster world of light?

Many dying people are instinctively calm and peaceful like my friend and parishioner so long ago. Later a dear brother-in-law went through death in the same way, moving forward firmly and quietly, knowing God enfolded him and that great welcome awaited him. One of his stepsons said in awe: "He taught us how to live. Now he is teaching us how to die."

Other people may need more help—hungering for reassurance, encouragement, closeness, and touching from others. Some of those left on earth may be able to move with relative peace through the wrench and shock of a loved one's death,

whereas others may need to face a longer grieving transition
while adjusting to a new way of life. We all respond in different,
sometimes surprising, ways. There is nothing whatever shameful
about grief. Tears are healthful; they are nature's merciful way
of helping us toward healing. Jesus wept at the news of the death
of his friend Lazarus, even though he knew Lazarus would live
again (John 11:33-35).

Jesus spoke poignant words about the death of the body,
which I quote at the beginning of this chapter. He asked us to
think of two tiny sparrows so insignificant they could be bought
in the marketplace for a penny. But when one of those birds
falls dead to the ground, it is never "apart from your Father"
(Matt. 10:29).

Some interpret this text as meaning that God chooses the
bird to die. I disagree. Jesus never taught that God chooses
death for us, especially for young people. Far too often it will
be said at funeral services or as an attempt to comfort the family: "Well, you know it was God's will," or "She was called to
heaven because God loved her so much," or "It is all for the
best," and so on. "All for the best" when a little child dies of
cancer? "God's will" that a wonderful young person dies in an
auto accident? "Called to heaven" when a man or woman in
strong midlife, supporting a family, drops dead with a heart
attack? Not according to Jesus! He healed people whenever and
wherever he could. Death will eventually come for us all because
it is nature's way to make room for new life. When it comes
too early through accident, devastating illness, killing, God will
indeed welcome into the world of light those who die. But God
will also grieve with us, as the tears of Jesus show us.

So when the sparrow falls, it is not God pointing a finger
and saying, "It is time for you to drop dead, little bird." Rather,
it means love enfolds that bird, which is never for one moment
"apart from your Father." So it is also with us. Whether our

death is timely after a long life or whether it is untimely, we are never alone, left without God's embrace.

Dying people who are still conscious may be able to speak to us of that enfolding love. Some experience a warm, welcoming light. Some tell us that there are loving presences in the room, perhaps friends or family members who have died earlier. Some may see angelic presences invisible to us but intensely present to the dying one.

If the dying ones are unconscious, we can speak to them, reminding them that they are not alone, that God's close presence and light surround them, that their spiritual body of light is gradually detaching from its physical clothing and wakening into a vaster realm where great joy and welcome await them. Though unconscious, their deep self will hear us and feel strengthened to move forward.

In my earlier book *Miracle,* I describe how my husband, who was in his last coma, spoke to me clearly in a dream: "This is like being in a swift stream in the water!" I heard no fear in his voice but rather an awed excitement. I had the image of the mighty Gulf Stream moving with warmth and power as an individual current through the Atlantic Ocean. I sensed that a similar warm, strong current was carrying my husband to his greater life. I felt that he wanted our encouraging thoughts and prayers to help release him even more fully to this gentle power.

Long before my husband's coma, he and I had shared our thoughts about his spiritual body of light being released gradually into an infinitely more spacious dimension—those dwelling places of which Jesus spoke. We believed together that he had always lived in that body of light, which had surrounded and permeated his mortal body since birth. He knew that as he became more physically frail, his spiritual body would become more powerful. At the point of death, his physical body, now no longer needed, would drop away.

My husband and I knew he would be welcomed with great love. He might need to rest for a while; prolonged illness tires the spirit as well as the body. But when ready, he would be invited not to fluffy white clouds and gold harps (he never liked lounging around) but to some intense, fascinating activity. He had always loved frontiers and horizons; exploring new places, new thoughts and ideas. Also, as a researcher he liked to discover how things connected and the ways apparent opposites related to each other both in science and in philosophy. In the vaster home, he would be able to discover and explore multifaceted ways the universe interconnected—ways unimaginable to him now. He had always had a wistful desire to paint and had begun painting in his last two years. Now he would have time and space to experiment with colors he had never seen. He had often wished he had learned to sail a boat. Now he could sail the seas of God!

We knew he would still love his family and the world where he had lived for seventy-seven years. Now he would learn to love us all in deeper ways and his flow of love to us would never cease, no matter how much he would grow. Though these ways of growing were beyond our imaginings and would reach dimensions for which we had no names, his closeness would still be with us. For example, a great astronomer or physicist works in realms of thought unimaginable to his two-year-old child. But every day that scientist holds that child closely in his or her heart and arms.

My husband would not grow closer to God, for God is already infinitely close to us, to every atom of creation. But he would grow in richer awareness of that all-permeating love and would learn fuller ways of responding to that love and becoming one with it.

It may not be possible or appropriate to explore all such thoughts with everyone who is going through the journey of dying.

Many are too tired; many others are new to these thoughts and find it hard to realize and respond. Others may simply not want to think about it. We should never push our thoughts and beliefs on anybody who is too tired to cope or who is in any way resistant.

It may be quite enough to be lovingly at their sides, holding their hands and, above all, listening to what they feel, think, or choose to share. We can respond to the feeling we sense beneath their words, and if they seem in any way open we can tell them gently that they can safely rest in God's hand, a hand that will guide them to a beautiful world of light. If they don't want words, we can inwardly envision them releasing their physical body, releasing their old life, moving into freedom where they will meet those who have always loved them and from whom they will never be separated again.

MEDITATION

"Into your hands I commend my spirit."
—Luke 23:46

Rest your body. Breathe fully, then naturally.... This is God's breath of eternal life... breathed on us forever, before and also after death....

If it feels natural for you, open your hands at rest on your lap in an act of receiving and releasing....

This is a meditation of release... release unto God.... Jesus' supreme prayer before death can also be expressed: "Into your hands I release my spirit."...

We can inwardly say this prayer not just at the time of death, but before any great change, any significant event, anything we hope for, anything we fear...before we sleep, as we rise each morning....

We can pray this prayer of release in the midst of a difficult experience...in the midst of creative work...in the midst of planning and preparing...in the midst of celebration...in the mist of anxiety...in the midst of confusion and uncertainty... in the midst of great tension....

This act of inner release clears the way for God's full action in our life, for our strength and inner healing to move with power....

If you are sensing inner fear or resistance at the thought of released trust, be gentle with your resistance. Force nothing.... Quietly take note of the inner block.... It is there because of early wounds or past abuses of your trust by other people.... This resistant closed door *is* the fear or pain.... God understands this....

Ask Christ the Healer to lay healing hands on the door...to enfold it with healing light....

The resistance may soon release its tension, or it may take longer. Sense what your bodily muscles are doing.... Is there tightness in your back...neck...shoulders...hands...feet? Our bodies hold the memories of inner wounds.... Force nothing.... If you feel ready, ask the Healer to touch these bodily areas with gentle, profound healing.... You may wish to touch them yourself....

Breathe deeply and slowly.... Relax your breathing.... God's breath of life is flowing into these tight areas....

Trust, release comes slowly. It may be enough for now to acknowledge the resistant door and simply look at it...try to hear what it is saying.... Christ listens with you.

As our trust heals and grows, we will be able to move into

our next experience knowing that the way is prepared for us, and Christ welcomes us as we go forth.

As you come forth from this meditation and face the next event of the day, see if you can say, "Into your hands I release my spirit."... See if you can say it tonight when you close your eyes to sleep... and tomorrow before you rise....

Gently massage your hands and face.... Stretch.... Go forth into your daily life.

EIGHT

Eternal Life Can Begin for Us Now

Jesus said to [Martha], "I am the resurrection and the life."
—John 11:25

ANNA WAS EIGHTY-FOUR when Jesus was born. She became one of the first witnessing disciples. We hear of her only in Luke's Gospel, which tells us her father's name, her tribal background, and her seven years of marriage before her long widowhood. She actually lived in the temple in Jerusalem, praying there night and day, and was considered to be a prophetess (Luke 2:36-37). Though Luke does not give the details, probably as a younger woman she had taken spiritual vows (as many widows did) and lived in one of the little rooms adjoining the Court of Women in the Temple. Perhaps she helped with the sewing and other domestic duties in and around the Temple as part of her devotional life. She also may have offered counseling to other women who came to worship.

Along with Simeon, she recognized the baby Jesus as the Chosen One, sent by God, when he was presented in the Temple: "At that moment she came, and began to praise God and to speak about the child to all who were looking for the redemption of Jerusalem" (Luke 2:38).

We do not hear much about Anna in sermons or liturgy. Only once have I seen her portrayed in art. She is overlooked in theological and spiritual teaching, as she was probably overlooked during her long, quiet life of service. But she has become a spiritual guide for me in my own later years:

She never left the temple but worshiped there ... night and day (Luke 2:37).

She never left the Temple! This implies far more than merely the great building where she lived and did her work. To me, this means eternal life, which can begin for us now.

I have known many men and women who have, once they entered, "never left the temple." Among them are scientists, teachers, artists, physicians, people in ministry and social justice work, office employees, salespersons, lawyers, insurance specialists, domestic workers, gardeners, engineers, construction workers, people in the military, homemakers, corporate managers, hospice workers. Some of these seem to have always been in the temple, having felt from birth the loving closeness of God. These are sometimes called the "Once-born." Others entered the temple as adolescents or in their middle years, or even when elderly.

Living in the temple does not mean being without faults and sins. It does not mean never making mistakes. I am sure Anna had her own share of human faults and limitations. It does not mean going nonstop to religious services nor does it mean reading the Bible all day or consciously praying every hour. Living in the temple is not the same as a life of rigid disciplinary religious rules or arrogant moral rules imposed on others in God's name.

Living in the temple, according to the Gospels, means entering and living in a freely chosen relationship with the Supreme, Transforming Love, whom we call God; it means abiding in that One as the branch abides in the living vine and relating to all others as equally loved by the One.

This inner wellspring, this center focal point, is the temple. This is where we may live, night and day, never leaving in spite of our faults and limitations. No one can take us from the temple. Nor do we take ourselves from the temple, no matter the sin or failure, so long as inner faithful love is at the center. Even if our love temporarily fails, we remain in the temple if our heart remains open and cries out for help. This is life eternal, which can begin this moment. We do not have to wait for bodily death to enter this temple, this "kingdom" as Jesus called it.

This is the good news Jesus came to tell in words and to share in deeds. But he also came to witness to its transforming power already at work among us. He recognized the presence of the temple, the kingdom, already enfolding the most unlikely people: Matthew, a tax-collector; Peter, a fisherman; James, Jesus' own brother; a good Samaritan (by definition a heretic); foreigners of another race and religious background such as the Syrophoenician woman and the Roman centurion; homemakers like Mary of Bethany; the crucified lawbreaker next to him on the cross.

All these people had much to learn, much growing to do. They all had their inner wounds. Many had made bad choices. But Jesus recognized in them an openness to love in their hearts, a longing for faith, a reaching out of trust, an awareness of someone greater than they enfolding them, a generosity of spirit.

Jesus brought his friend Lazarus back to life not simply because he loved his friend but also to bear witness that eternal life with God is a present reality. Eternal life does not need to wait fifty years for a Jubilee Year or until the end of time and the Final Judgment. Eternal life begins now and will never die.

I wonder if this is why Jesus did not discuss the specific details of life after death. He saw eternal life as a wholeness, a continuum with no dividing categories. He knew eternal life was the unbroken relationship with God on this side of death and on the other. It is the eternal *now*.

Jesus was saying this to the Samaritan woman at the well (John 4:1-27). He was breaking every possible religious and cultural taboo when he talked with her there. He was a rabbi, a teacher of sacred things. He not only was talking to a woman but was talking to her alone! Moreover, she was a woman of extremely dubious reputation and a Samaritan! Samaritans were heretics. They did not believe that the temple in Jerusalem was the true center of worship. A special mountain in their land, a much holier place, was where they gathered to worship God.

When the woman pointed out this difference in their beliefs, Jesus made a radical remark that would have horrified the orthodox in Israel *and* in Samaria:

> *Jesus said to her, "Woman, believe me, the hour is coming when you will worship the Father neither on this mountain nor in Jerusalem.... But the hour is coming, and is now here, when the true worshipers will worship the Father in spirit and truth"* (John 4:21, 23, my emphasis).

Jesus was speaking of the true center, the living temple, never destroyed, forever open to God.

In the profoundest sense, we are never out of that temple. We may think we have left God, but God never for a moment leaves us. I have been struck by a strange remark Jesus made concerning children: "Their angels continually see the face of my Father in heaven" (Matt. 18:10). We are all God's children. Is the innermost part of us—our ultimate soul as God first created it—at this moment looking on God's face? Is it true that no matter where we are on our life's path, the essential part of who we are has never left God and forever looks on the face of God?

If so, then the firm foundation beneath us is mightier than the whole universe:

> *Where can I go from your spirit?*
> *Or where can I flee from your presence?*
> *If I ascend to heaven, you are there;*
> *if I make my bed in Sheol, you are there.*
> *If I take the wings of the morning*
> *and settle at the farthest limits of the sea,*
> *even there your hand shall lead me,*
> *and your right hand shall hold me fast.*
> (Psalm 139:7-10)

I had a powerful parable experience some years ago that showed me we are never really away from God's center. I arrived a day early at a retreat house where I was to teach at a conference. A labyrinth had just been dug in the grounds. Though I had read and studied the meanings of a labyrinth, I had never walked through one. This would be a good, meditative experience for me, I decided, especially when preparing spiritually for the conference beginning the next day.

The rain had stopped, so I walked through the wet grass to the freshly laid-out labyrinth paths and entered the opening. It was a very large labyrinth since the grounds were extensive, and I looked forward to the hour ahead of me. I would meditate on my life's journey while moving very slowly to the center.

In fewer than ten steps I was standing in the center!

I stood there, dazed. How had I gotten there? I was reasonably sure I had not been airlifted by some angel. I was equally sure I had not fallen into a trance and forgotten time. After a moment of rational thought, I realized that since the ground was still wet after the early morning drizzle, probably the mounds of earth separating the paths had dampened down and I had inadvertently walked through them rather than staying within them.

Should I go back to the beginning and start again? I sensed that something more was being told me than just the result of flattened earth mounds. I waited quietly. I heard nothing, but within me an answer was forming:

God's heart is not a goal to be reached.
Everyone's deep soul is already there forever, safe.

I stood there, awed, as the implications sank in. Should I return to the entrance by the long, winding path? I decided to do that at another time. I had received for this day what God wanted me to know.

That evening, while going over my notes, I came across a quote I had copied from some anthology years before. I can no longer find the documentary reference, but I remember it was from a second-century apocryphal writing concerning a dialogue with Jesus:

They said to him: "What is the place to which we shall go?"
The Lord said: "As for the place which you shall be able to reach, you are standing on it."[1]

I began to laugh. This, of course, was the whole point of that universally loved book and movie *The Wizard of Oz*. In spite of tornadoes, magic shoes, far countries, witches, wizards, haunted forests, castles of doom, yellow brick roads, and faithful comrades of strange appearance, Dorothy was simultaneously (without realizing it) safe in her own home. She had never left it. Her wish was already granted.

But is the journey then unimportant, unessential? What does it matter whether or not we walk the labyrinth if we are already at its center? Were Dorothy's adventures just a foolish, melodramatic dream with no point? Why do we struggle through life in this world if we are already at home with God?

The journey matters because only through the journey do we become aware of where we already are. Only when we become aware can we freely choose what we truly want. Only when we make the free choice of responding with love to the eternal heart and home that enfolds us do we enter into a full, mature relationship with God.

This is the breathlessly awesome risk God has taken. We are not to lie forever as unborn babies, forever receiving. We are to grow up, full sons and daughters, knowing what we receive, choosing how to respond to the Heart that holds us.

To choose to live in the temple with intentionality and full response is not vague idealism. It is solid, practical, and intertwined with our daily life. Here are some ways we can live through each day with awareness within the temple:

Waking and rising: Respond gently to the act of waking. Sense that you are resting in God's heart and that through the day ahead that heart will guide and empower you. Think of God's breath of life flowing at this moment through every part of your body, filling each cell and organ with vitality. Breathe slowly and deeply. When ready, stretch gently and rise.

Eating and drinking: During the Lord's Supper we pray, "Pour out your Holy Spirit upon this bread and this cup."[2] We can bring the same essential inner prayer to all that we eat and drink. All the gifts of life through our five senses can become to us sacraments of God's immediate presence. Think gratefully of our earth's body with its colors, fragrances, tastes, and textures.

Think also of those who hunger in the body and/or in the heart. How can we reach out to them this day?

Facing the day: "I go to prepare a place for you" (John 14:2), Jesus said to his friends. Christ prepares us not only for death but also for the next experience of our day. Ask the Christ to go ahead of you into that appointment, that office, that task, that conversation to fill it with healing and light. Ask that when you enter that moment, that place, later in the day, you will feel welcomed and guided.

During the day: Often throughout the day, remind yourself that you are in the temple and God's love surrounds you now. Sense the light of that love flowing into all parts of your body: hands, feet, arms, legs, eyes, ears, heart, brain. Thank these bodily parts for their faithful service. Touch them gently and warmly. Listen to them when they signal stress, fatigue, or anxiousness. God speaks to us through our bodies about imbalances in our lives.

Nurturing pauses: Take time throughout the day to relax the bodily muscles, to breathe slowly and quietly, knowing that each breath is God's breath of life flowing into us. Gaze out the window at the sky, a tree, a green leaf, a bird's flight, raindrops. Think of God's light opening like a flower within your heart and flowing through your body. These moments are little sabbaths, holy spaces, within our temple.

Relating to others: When meeting others by telephone, e-mail, letter, face-to-face, think of God's tenderness surrounding and filling the other person. Pray that you both will be guided during the encounter. If the other person presents a problem for you, is perhaps hard to like, ask God to help you see the hidden, unspoken wounds in the other and pray for his or her healing. At the same time, ask that your own healthy borders be strengthened so that you may not be drained or encroached upon. These borders are not defensive, rigid walls but radiant, permeable strength.

Or ask the Risen Christ to stand between you and the other, not as a barrier but as the Healer whose transforming power flows to you both.

Healing inner wounds: Ask God to help you become aware of your own wounds and inner pain: anger, grief, loneliness, shame, disappointment, stress, fatigue, hurting memories. Look with compassion at these inner "children." You may not have time during a busy day to encounter them at depth but note their presence and ask the Risen Christ to touch each one with healing love. Remember to return to them later and listen to them in God's presence. What do these hurts want to tell you? Ask for guidance in how to help them heal at depth.

Celebrating your gifts: Take a few minutes during the day to taste joy and gratitude that you have felt the strength equal to your task, that you have been given wisdom and intelligence to solve a problem, that you have felt love for another and been empowered to help that person, that you have seen a situation with clearness and known how to tell the truth in love. This celebration is not boastfulness; it is healthy gratitude for being a part of God's beautiful creation. This is hard to do. So much of our spiritual teaching has promoted false humility and low self-esteem (even self-loathing), which is an insult to God, who delights in our growth and gifts.

At day's end: Reflect on what has helped or hurt you through the day. Release these events into God's healing heart. Reflect briefly on the people you have met this day. Release each one into God's healing hands. Gently breathe in the love and peace that holds you and surrounds you. Release your bodily muscles into that safety and strength. Pray the prayer of Jesus: "Into your hands I commend my spirit" (Luke 23:46). Let God's mystery of sleep enfold you.

These suggestions are not meant to be rigid rules. No true relationship should be governed by rigid rules, much less our relationship with the living God, which is our temple. These suggestions are general guidelines for ways to open ourselves more fully to the presence of the One who loves and breathes life eternal into us. We should not burden ourselves with guilt if we do not remember to open ourselves to God in these ways every day. Jesus always wanted to release people from burdens, especially spiritual burdens. Frequently he rebuked the Pharisees, who overloaded people with religious pressure and guilt.

Discover your own way of keeping your awareness of God alive and growing. Some people respond best when they have set times for prayer and meditation. Others, who like to keep their bodies moving, find their closeness to God when walking, running, swimming, bicycle riding, and the like. What I have called a "parable walk" can be especially helpful. We start our walk with no agenda. We simply ask God to show us something that is important for us in our spiritual growth. God will always show us something. It may be the shape of a tree or what a bird or squirrel is doing or the face of a flower, the pattern on a stone, a house, a person walking by. It may be a fragrance, a sound, a texture we touch, a warm gust of wind. Whatever it is, we will know this is the message to us. We will recognize its significance. We may not know its full meaning right away, but later that meaning will unfold for us.

Some, like myself, prefer responding to God through a mixture of ongoing prayer throughout the day and occasional longer, more focused times set aside for deep prayer and communion with God. This is the way I respond best to other people too—hugs, smiles, comments, questions, conversation through the day but also occasions set aside (perhaps weekly) when I sit or walk with a person for a time of depth sharing.

As we live, grow, learn, and love in our temple of eternal life, we will begin to notice changes within us. Some may come quickly, others very gradually. I don't know where I read or heard a wise spiritual leader say that the Sermon on the Mount (Matthew 5–7) is meant to be descriptive, not prescriptive. What Jesus said to us is not so much orders given from above as descriptions of what happens within us when we enter a deep relationship with the living God. For example, it becomes increasingly natural to pray for an enemy rather than being obedient to a distasteful order through gritted teeth and willpower (Matt. 5:43-45).

As the Spirit of the living God grows within us, increasingly we are inwardly transformed, often at levels far beyond our conscious perception.

We will notice eventually within us a wider, fuller tenderness and reverence for the world around us—its people, nature, all that the world holds.

We will experience a growing ability to face and reach out to the pain of those around us without crushing despair. We can weep freely but in hopefulness.

We will feel a need to speak the truth clearly but without judgment or arrogance. Our anger becomes clearer and more honest, clean of bitterness.

We will have a richer sense of the beauty and wonder of the world and the sacramental power of our five senses.

We will enjoy more laughter and delight. We will notice a growing reservoir of inner peace, centeredness.

Perhaps above all, we will realize more and more that we are indeed the beloved of God, not insignificant atoms in an indifferent universe; not mere miserable sinners awaiting divine wrath and judgment; not instruments to be picked up, used, then dropped by God; not slaves or even servants of God.

Who does Jesus say we are?

"I do not call you servants any longer.... I have called you friends" (John 15:15).

We will serve God, yes, but not as servants. We will serve as the beloved serve one another. Thomas Traherne, English pastor and poet, expressed it this way three hundred and fifty years ago:

Too weak and feeble to express
The true mysterious depths of blessedness.
I am His image, and His friend,
His son, bride, glory, temple, end.[3]

I am writing this chapter a few days before Christmas. In spite of the world's unspeakable pain, candles are lit and lights are shining from the windows. It is Christmas. It is also Easter. The two cannot be separated. The Incarnation and the Resurrection are one and the same. What is this Oneness saying?

The Light has become one with the lightless and illumined it.
The Strongest has become one with the weakest and empowered it.
The Vastest has become one with the smallest and glorified it.
The Blissful has become one with the agonized and healed it.
The Adored has become one with the cursed and loved it.
The Wholeness has become one with the fragmented and united it.
The Life has become one with the death and resurrected it.
Was this the inner cry of Mary as she gave birth to Jesus?
Was this the heart's cry of that other Mary when Jesus spoke her name in the garden of the graves?
Easter, Christmas, all our days of life and life beyond death are gathered up into the One everlasting day that is God's heart.

Can there be any day but this,
Though many suns to shine endeavor?

We count three hundred, but we miss:
There is but one, and that one ever.[4]
(George Herbert, 1593–1663)

NOTES

FRONTISPIECE

Saint Clement of Alexandria, *Address to the Greeks* in *The New Christian Year*. Chosen by Charles Williams (London: Oxford University Press, 1941), 103.

TWO: Death Is Not the End

1. *Meister Eckhart: A Modern Translation*, tr. Raymond Bernard Blakney (New York: Harper & Row, 1941), 74.

FOUR: What Is Heaven?

1. "Jerusalem the Golden." Lyrics by Bernard of Cluny (Twelfth Century). Music by Alexander Ewing. *The Pilgrim Hymnal* (Cleveland, OH: The Pilgrim Press, 1931), p. 309, verse 3.

2. Robert Browning, "Prospice," in *Browning's Shorter Poems*, selected and edited by Franklin T. Baker (New York: The Macmillan Co., 1917).

3. Mark 2:16; Luke 8:43-48; Luke 13:10-16; Mark 10:46-52.

FIVE: What Is Hell?

1. Leslie D. Weatherhead, *The Christian Agnostic* (London: Hodder and Stoughton, 1965), 222.

2. *Acts of Pilate*, in *The Apocryphal New Testament*, trans. by M. R. James (Oxford: Clarendon Press 1955), 134, 135, 136, 139.

EIGHT: Eternal Life Can Begin for Us Now

1. *The Dialogue of the Savior* in *The Other Gospels:*
   Non-Canonical Gospel Texts, edited by Ron Cameron
   (Philadelphia: The Westminster Press, 1982), 47. The
   translation I have differs slightly from the Cameron version.

2. The phrase "Pour out your Holy Spirit upon this bread and
   this cup" appears in the liturgy for Holy Communion in
   many denominational worship books.

3. Thomas Traherne, "Love," verse 4. *From George Herbert*
   and the Seventeenth-Century Religious Poets. Selected and
   edited by Mario A. Di Cesare (New York: W. W. Norton &
   Co., 1978), 193.

4. George Herbert, "Easter," last verse. From *George Herbert*
   and the Seventeenth-Century Religious Poets. Selected and
   edited by Mario A. Di Cesare (New York: W. W. Norton &
   Co., 1978), 18.

ABOUT THE AUTHOR

FLORA SLOSSON WUELLNER, a retired ordained minister of the United Church of Christ, is well-known throughout the United States and Europe for her writings and retreat leadership that focus on the inner healing God offers freely through Christ. She has been involved in a specialized ministry of spiritual renewal for over 40 years and has written 14 books on individual and communal healing.

Flora served as adjunct faculty member for 12 years at Pacific School of Religion, Berkeley, California, in the field of spiritual wholeness. Educated at the University of Michigan and at Chicago Theological Seminary, she has served pastorates in Wyoming, Idaho, and Illinois. Flora currently lives in Fair Oaks, California.

OTHER TITLES BY FLORA SLOSSON WUELLNER
FROM UPPER ROOM BOOKS

Enter by the Gate:
Jesus' 7 Guidelines When Making Hard Choices

Feed My Shepherds:
Spiritual Healing and Renewal for Those in Christian Leadership

Forgiveness, the Passionate Journey:
Nine Steps of Forgiving Through Jesus' Beatitudes

Miracle:
When Christ Touches Our Deepest Need

Prayer and Our Bodies

Prayer, Stress, and Our Inner Wounds

Release:
Healing from Wounds of Family, Church, and Community

For more information about these titles,
visit www.upperroom.org/bookstore,
or call 1-800-972-0433.